Dear Hal,
Yours Pud

Compiled and edited by

Theo Stibbons

POPPYLAND
PUBLISHING

Designed & typeset in 11/13.2pt
Times New Roman by
Poppyland Publishing, Cromer
NR27 9AN

Printed by The Complete
Product Company

ACKNOWLEDGEMENTS

Since the discovery of the letters which make up the greater part of this book, several people have assisted in my research. I am grateful to all the members of my family who have assisted and particularly to Ray's son and daughter–in–law, Laurence and Margaret Randall. Staff and resources of the Imperial War Museum, the Commonwealth War Graves Commission and the National Archives have all been of great help, as has Ian Hook of the Essex Regimental Museum in Chelmsford. Thanks to Neil Storey with some matters of identification. My colleague Hilary Faulkner kindly undertook the translation of the German cards

My wife Melanie has helped greatly over the years, with comments on the text and presentation. She and my brother Peter and his wife Brenda have also assisted me in further research including visits to the battlefields of northern France.

PICTURE CREDITS

Unless otherwise indicated, the pictures have all come from the family collection, many being found with the letters.

National Archives: 22, 27, 28, 29, 32, 50, 51, 56, 59, 60, 63, 64, 78, 79, 88
With the 10th Essex in France: 86

Images overlaid on Google maps on the World Wide Web by agreement with The National Archives

THE LETTERS

In these days when families are on the move so much it is perhaps rare to find by chance a record from the past. Yet there is no diminution of interest in family stories; indeed it is even greater now in the age of the Internet and the World Wide Web with the ability to access many more records. When I started researching the background to these letters over twenty years ago, there were far less sources available and facilities such as the on–line access to The National Archives has certainly made investigation much easier.

My grandfather Harold Randall died in 1974. He didn't throw anything away that he thought might be useful! The family shop in Cromer had been his home and many photographs and papers had been put away in the loft and then moved to another family house. The letters he and his family received from his brother Ray had received slightly better treatment, being packed carefully in a suitcase..........

Back to more recent times. When I first visited the First World War battlefields referred to in the letters in the 1980s, there was a reasonable level of interest in family history in those tragic and yet courageous times. Now there is a constant stream of enquiry from the next generation, with study of the First World War part of many classroom history lessons and the ability to explore without upsetting deeply hidden nightmares in the memories of our grandparents.

Likewise this book does not stand on its own. Alongside you'll find part of the story on the Internet, with colour photos, video and panoramas to the places visited as part of the research. Through agreement with The National Archives you can also see the actual maps from the War Diaries of the 10th Essex Regiment plotted on top of satellite imagery of the ground today. The maps have been georegistered to match the modern mapping on the Web and as the physical evidence on the ground gradually disappears, these maps will enable you to see where the men of the 10th Essex stood their ground and then went "over the top".

The letters have been reproduced as written including spelling errors and grammatical errors except where the meaning or understanding of the letter may not have been clear.

Theo Stibbons
July 2008

Contents

The Letters 3

Introduction 5

September 1914 7

Training 9

From the Front 21

Advance on the Somme 77

Back to Blighty 99

Index 112

The web site *www.poppyland.co.uk* has a "Support and Resources" button which will lead to a number of pages specially compiled in association with this title. In particular you can see mapping of the principal sites mentioned in the text and overlay maps from the official War Diary of the 10th Essex.

Also from Poppyland Publishing:
Grandad's War: The First World War Diary of Horace Reginald Stanley
ISBN 978 0 946 148 83 7
by Juliet and Heather Brodie

INTRODUCTION

Ray Randall 1895 - 1977

Raymond Edward Ralph Randall, known as 'Pudlo' to his close family, was the youngest of the five sons – Wilfred, Theodore, Reginald, Harold and Raymond – of Robert and Clara Randall of Cromer, Norfolk. There were also three sisters, Mabel, Sybil and Enid, the last of whom was younger than Ray. All five brothers served during the First World War at various times and in varying ways.

Ray received his nickname from a favourite story told to the children by their father Robert. The story involved the character "Pudlo suck–a–thumb". Ray was christened this by the other children.

When Ray left school he first worked for Chevertons, the printer in Bond Street, Cromer, then at their office and workshop in Sheringham. He then moved to the East Coast Motor Company back at Cromer. It was from there he volunteered for the army.

This book contains the extant letters he sent to his brother, Harold (Hal) , to his mother and father and one or two others to brothers and sisters. It also contains entries from his diary. To help understand the context, quotations from some of the official battalion histories and other accounts are included.

The 10th Essex Regiment in which Ray served was a 'Service' Battalion meaning that it was raised as a direct result of Kitchener's 'Your Country Needs You' appeal.

It was part of the 53rd Infantry Brigade. Other Battalions in this Brigade were the 6th Royal Berkshires, 8th Norfolks and 8th Suffolks. The 53rd Brigade, along with the 54th and 55th Brigades, formed the 18th Division.

On July 1st 1916, the first day of the Battle of the Somme, the 18th Division was to be one of the most successful Divisions on the whole of the Western Front. This may be seen in no small way due to the training they received under Lieutenant General Sir Ivor Maxse KCB, CVO, DSO.

Robert and Clara Randall and their family early in the First World War. Those with uniforms wear them for the photograph.
Back row, from the left: Sergeant Theodore of the 5th Norfolks, Robert Randall, Enid, Wilfred, Harold and Raymond of the 10th Essex. Reginald was on service in Egypt.
Front row: Mabel, Nellie (Mrs. Theodore), Clara with the young Robert, Mabel (Mrs Wilfred), Sybil. The sisters were teachers and nurses.

SEPTEMBER 1914

It all began in September 1914.

In the main the battalions were representative of their counties. The 8th Norfolks and the 8th Suffolks were especially strong territorially and a large overflow of volunteers from these counties found its way into other battalions in the Divisions.

Volunteers at Cromer, on parade after recruitment for the army. Close examination of the cap badge suggests these men are from the Gloucestershire Yeomanry, posted to Cromer before all receiving their uniforms.

Volunteers on parade, probably after arrival in Norwich. They would spend the first night as enlisted men on the floor of the Agricultural Hall.

This was how Ray came to be in the 10th Essex. He had enlisted in the 8th Norfolks but was transferred, to help form the 10th Essex, after only three weeks.

*Shorncliffe Camp,
Kent.*

The Division, on assembly, represented very little more than a collection of several thousand men, full of enthusiasm and keen to do their best, but without uniforms, equipment or arms, and it was many weeks before these deficiencies were rectified.

The 10th Essex, in common with all other units, had these initial difficulties to overcome. The men were exceedingly good material, being fifty per cent of them recruits from Stratford, Leyton, Poplar, Bethnal Green and Walthamstow. Another 25 per cent were from the rural districts of Essex and the remaining 25 per cent came from Norfolk and Suffolk. This amalgam of good, yet varied, East Coast stock made a first–rate fighting unit.

The battalion was formed at Shorncliffe Camp, near Folkestone, Kent, in September 1914. The first sign of the battalion coming into being was a bell tent with a board outside with the words 'Orderly Room 10th Essex' chalked on it.

The officer of the battalion made his mark in these difficult first days.

Captain Heppell had been placed in command of the battalion pending the appointment of a senior officer. It was only a week or two before that he had been a junior subaltern, but now he was faced with an emergency which has tested many old and more experienced campaigners. The men were hungry. The commissariat arrangements were not equal to the requirements and so it came about that a deputation of indignant soldiers – but a few days before independent working men – waited upon him and told, in lurid language, the urgency of their need. Patient explanation was of no avail; they wanted food. At last exasperated at their insistence, the harassed captain threw off his tunic and, if he could not give them rations, offered to fight them one after another, beginning with the ringleader. This timely exhibition of pugilistic ability in the British officer had a salutary effect. Combat was declined and thereafter the men of the 10th Essex were content to understand that the best that was possible was being done for them in abnormal circumstances.

TRAINING

Very few of the letters sent by Ray during his training are dated but they are believed to be in the correct order and with, in some cases, an idea of when they were written. Ray enlisted on September 4th 1914 in Norwich, into the 8th Norfolk Regiment. As we have explained, he was then transferred to the newly formed 10th Essex Regiment.

Shorncliffe, Kent
Dear Hal,
I was very glad to get your letter and thanks very much for the fags. I haven't got any equipment yet nor rifle. I was put into the Essex Regt because the Norfolks are up to full strength but it doesn't matter what Battalion I'm in. Would you mind collecting my present off old W.J. Miller and forwarding it as I haven't been payed (sic) yet and am getting hard up. We have got the only brigade of the R.F.A. in England down here. I saw the cliffs of France on Sunday from Folkestone and also the search lights which sweep the Straits of Dover all night. Theo, Mabs, Wilf have all written to me and I'm now going to write to them. I must now say ta–ta as I haven't much time before the next parade.
With love from Pudlo Raymond.

'A' Company,
10th Essex Regt
St Martins Plain,
Shorncliffe
Kent
Dear Hal,
Sorry haven't written before but have been very busy drilling. Have not got my uniform yet I hope to get it some day. They haven't started picking out our Company yet so I have to drill just the same as the others but expect it won't be long now before I have a shift. Hope you are still taking care of Nellie and you might ask her about my fish and chip supper and when I'm going to get it. We went down to bathing parade this morning about 4–30a.m. but I did not go in because it was 'too blooming cold'. You might send me Theo's address and also Wilf's and Mabel's as I have forgotten them. I don't think I've any more to say as I've put all the news in the other letters so goodbye for the present.
Your loving pal, Pudlo
P.S. Don't forget to write soon.

In October the 10th Essex left Shorncliffe for Hyderabad Barracks, Colchester, and in passing through Liverpool Street Station were the subject of a great demonstration of welcome by relatives and friends. So much so that some were left behind when the train steamed out for Colchester, but they followed later under the kindly supervision of a party of officers specially detailed for the purpose. The early days of Colchester were spent in the blue clothing which became the familiar badge of distinction between soldier and civilian, but the wearing of which was not relished by the ardent volunteer, who longed for the distinctive khaki of war–time renown. The recruitment of the band was a notable feat; the visit of a cornet player to Wivenhoe on a Saturday evening, an eloquent and forceful speech to the local band, and ere the night had passed the 10th Essex had a right loyal company to inspire all ranks with martial music (see page 114).

Ray was allocated to 'A' Company and served with it throughout his war service.

The companies had taken on their own individual and distinctive characters under their respective commanders. They each inhabited separate blocks of the barracks, and were commonly considered to take precedence according to their distance from the officers' mess. Anyhow Major Wheatly had assured himself of a short walk to his parade ground in the morning by assuming command of 'A' Company, and had collected around him a select lot of young men of the highest respectability. 'A' Company's orderly room was the Mayfair of Hyderabad Barracks.

The Battalion passed through varied phases of training.......... As field training progressed the influence of the divisional commander, Major–General Maxse, became more and more marked........

The next letter is on Soldiers' Christian Association headed paper.

Hyderabad Barracks
Colchester
October 12th 1914
Dear Hal,
Very pleased to receive your letter. We have done 75mls route marching in the last four days, so you can guess my feet are getting pretty tender. We are still waiting for our uniforms, I expect they are trying to grow them. Mabs is coming down this Sunday so I shall try and get the day off and see her. I've seen several of the Cromer gang down here both Terriers and Kitcheners, the 8th Norfolks are opposite to us, in the same grounds. It's just the same down here as regards to lights the town is practably (sic) in darkness. Theo has written to our C.O. but am afraid it is not possible to get transferred from the Regulars to the Terriers. Theo and I wondered that Con Moulton didn't join the 5th Norfolks instead of the 4th. We have some fine swimming baths at the Barracks the only drawback is that they have no means of warming them and just now the water is inclined to be chilly, but if you don't go in they make you a prisoner and give you three days C.B.* I don't think I've any more to write about except that I haven't had any C.B. yet.
Yours Pud

* confined to barracks

Ray makes reference in this letter to the blackout that was obviously in place in many east coast towns in anticipation of Zeppelin raids.

The next extract is from Ray's letter (right) with the diagram of the 'new' way of making trenches. It explains how the earth was not to be banked in front of the trench, as doing this attracted artillery fire.

Hyderabad Barracks
Colchester
Dear Hal,
Thanks very much for your letter which I read in the train going up to town. The pheasant which I received was lovely and went down a treat. I didn't see Georgy* the other day but I heard about his visit. Haven't heard anything more about the dispatch riding yet but haven't given up hope yet. I hope to be home for Xmas but don't know how long I shall get. We have started digging trenches now and its pretty hard graft, they are on an entirely new principal (sic). I don't think I've any more news now after my graphic drawing.
With much love,
Yours, Pud

* King George V

Hyderabad Barracks
Colchester
Dear Hal,
Thanks very much for letter. Yes I am a first class navvy now, and shall be able to get a job on the council when I come out of the army. I haven't heard any more about the Dispatch work yet. We are going to have a week off on leave and each company is having its leave each week, but no one will be allowed out of barracks on Xmas Day and Boxing Day. I've heard we are going on the 29th Dec. but am not sure yet. We have had a full week this week, on Monday we went to Clacton– on–Sea and came home the following day, we slept in barns the Monday night with one blanket each. Clacton is 21miles from Colchester. On Wednesday we went to Brightlingsea (which is 11 miles there and 22 in all) and back. Thursday we went out to the trenches we are making and slept in them the night returning home the Friday morning and finishing for the day at 12o'clock. We were on the butts all last week and

I let off about 60 rounds but am not a very good shot yet, I generally get about 5 shots out of seven at 500yds. We are going to have another beautiful 6 days next week, we start on Monday for Harwich and I expect stop there the night, I don't know the rest of the programme yet, but I expect it will be just as cushy. Hoping you are keeping fit. Love to all at home,
Yours, Raymond.
P.S. Have just heard that I'm certain to be home on the 29th Dec., this is the order the companies are going home in:– B Coy. Dec.9th to the 15th Dec., C Coy Dec.16th to the 22nd Dec., A Coy. Dec.29th to the 4th Jan., D Coy Jan. 5th to the 11th Jan.1915. So you see all the companies will be in barracks for Xmas.

This letter gives an idea of the intensive training that the men of 'Kitchener's Army' had to go through. The next three letters were written before Ray went on leave. They continue to give details of the type of training given to infantrymen.

Hyderabad Barracks
Colchester
Dear Hal,
So sorry to hear you have been ill, you don't take enough care of yourself you know but am glad to hear you are getting better and hope you will soon be quite well. I have had a rotten arm for the last week and at times I feel like getting a chopper and cutting it off. I'm glad to see by the paper that they haven't blown Cromer up yet but I expect it was a close thing. We start our last month firing on Monday and then we go onto Brigade drill, they have served us out with another suit of blues to keep our khaki clean. We went to a little village called Manningtree the other day about 12 miles out of Colchester and the people there treated us very well, they made two or three urns of coffee and gave us apples and cakes. I don't think I have anything else to write now.
With best love to all, Yours Pudlo.

Hyderabad Barracks
Colchester
Dear Hal,
Thanks ever so much for the pipe, its a little beauty and also for the good wishes. I am getting on gradually with my shooting and generally manage to score 15 out of twenty on the 500 yd target which is 4ft square with a 12in bull. We are now on rapid fire course, the targets for this are up 5 seconds and down 10 seconds in which time you have to load, and get your shot off in 5 seconds. Am afraid I shan't be a marksman nor a 1st class shot but might happen to rank as a second class. We have had a Zepplin (sic) scare here and have been on patrol duty two nights with loaded rifles and had to go without lights for three nights but nothing very exciting happened. It looks as if Reg. may see some life yet, I see the Indians out there have begun to wake the Turks up. I'm jolly glad you are better and hope you will soon be fit and well again. I will shut up now as am now going to have a bath.
With best love to all, Yrs, Pud.

Brother Reg, with the Norfolk Yeomanry prior to the war.

12

Hyderabad Barracks
Colchester
Dear Hal,
Thanks ever so much for the baccy which will last me ever so long. I shall be able to tell you all the news when I come home. Hope you are in the best of health and are not over working yourself. I'm afraid I shall have to make my letter as short as yours to catch the post.
With best love to all, Yours, Pud.

After having what was no doubt a very welcome leave at home in Cromer, Ray went back to Hyderabad Barracks in Colchester to continue his training. The next seven letters are all from there, before he moved to Wiltshire for Divisional Training.

Hyderabad Barracks
Colchester
Tuesday
Dear Hal,
Thanks ever so much for the fags. I went up to Wilf's last weekend and also had the pleasure of seeing Pa. We are leaving tomorrow on our 170 miles march and I am feeling quite fit for it. Am sending off one of my photos, Mabs made me have it done else I don't suppose it would have been done yet. We have just been served with 120 rounds of ball cartridges and are absolutely fit for active service, so I hope we shan't be long before we go across the water. The drawing on the side is supposed to represent one of our long bayonetts (sic), they are only sharp one side and have an edge like a razor all the way down and the middle is scooped out.
With love to all, Yours Pud.

The drawing referred to on this page.

The Essex Regiment
10th Battalion

At the end of April 1915, there was a brigade march into Suffolk. First an eighteen miles tramp to Ipswich, where the reception was most hospitable, then on to Woodbridge, Hollesley Bay and back again by way of Woodbridge to Ipswich .... On the march back to Colchester the 54th Brigade was passed, going out for the hard training which the 53rd Brigade had endured, and General Maxse was there too, to take the salute as the brigades tramped along. The 53rd came back hardened campaigners, having marched one hundred miles in seven days.

From a pig yard,
Hollesley
Suffolk
Sunday
Dear Hal,
Have just received your welcome letter. This is the first chance I have had of writing a letter and don't know whether I shall be able to post it today. Our Brigade is billeted in farms, barns, stables and so far this is the worst place we have been in. I had nice billet at Ipswich and bacon and eggs for breakfast. Our programme so far has been:–
Wednesday, march to Ipswich, Thursday, march and skirmish to Woodbridge, and our Coy. on Outpost Duty all night. Friday march and skirmish to Hollesley Bay and guard

duty for me. Saturday, skirmish in the afternoon from 1–30pm to 6–30pm and another march and skirmish at 12pm to 7–30am. Sunday morning total mileage so far is 80 miles. I shall have to post this on the way back as it is impossible to get a stamp round here. You might tell Ma I shall be back in barracks by Thursday. Am sending a little copy of the periscope which Pa gave me the money to buy you might show it to Pa. Thanks ever so much for the fags you sent. I think this is all just now.
Yrs, Pud.
P.S. The new bayonet is 6 inches longer than the old.

Following this detailed letter the next one is interesting for different reasons. The first part of it is typed. It is reproduced here exactly as typed with the error in Zeppelin.

No.17812
Hyderabad barracks
Dear Hal,
Have got a job at brigade office as telephone operator and am having a cushy time. We have had several Zepelin scares and also had two bombs dropped here but they didn't do much dammage just broke a few windows. I must stop typing now as my arm is getting tired and it has taken me about two hrs. to do this little bit. I just had a message through to say that seven German Aeroplanes were expected over tonight so I expect we shall have some fun. I shan't need to buy any more paper or envelopes.
With best love to all, Yrs. Pud.

A typed letter to his father, "Pa" Randall.

Hyderabad Barracks
Colchester
Dear Pa,
Thanks very much for your letter which was very welcome. I am growing very fat and lazy am afraid this life isn't improving me very much I expect I shall feel it when I go back to the ranks and have to wear the full pack again .... I am getting quite expert at taking messages off the phone and one has to write very quickly when receiving a call especially when a ratty old Colonel gets on the line, you would think some of them were bargees by their language.........
With best love to all, Your loving Son, Raymond.

This "cushy" job didn't last long. The next two letters had a printed heading – a legacy of the "cushy" job.

10th (Service) Bn The Essex Regt.,
Hyderabad Barracks,
Colchester
Dear Hal,
Thanks ever so much for the baccy and letter. I have to start pen scratching again as they have taken me off my nice little job I thought they got jealous when they (sic) I wasn't doing much. I haven't they (sic) slightest idear (sic) when we are moving of

course there are plenty of rumours flying about. We are now on the last stages of Battalion training and shall have to shift somewhere else to do Divisional Training because there isn't room here. There was a yarn about us going to Egypt and that it was in the "Army and Navy Gazzette"(sic) but as I haven't seen the paper I don't know whether it is correct. I sent my watch along to see if you can ajust (sic) his internal works I don't know what is gone wrong with him, but I happened to let it down while out trenching one night.
Hoping you are keeping fit, Yrs Pud.

It is not clear why there are so many spelling errors in this letter; perhaps Ray was in a hurry or just tired. It is not typical, generally his letters are very well written, even those from the front line trenches.

The next letter, again on headed notepaper, records what appears to be an amazing incident that occurred during Brigade training. Perhaps it often happened.

10th (Service) Bn.
The Essex Regt.,
Hydrabad Barracks,
Colchester
Dear Hal,
Thanks ever so much for the ticker, what was wrong with mine? I expect you have been having a rough time of it with Pa in bed and hope you have been keeping fit. We have just had three of our chaps wounded you see it happened on one of our Brigade Training days and we were firing blanks and somehow one of the chaps shoved a live cartridge into his rifle and buzzed it off and it passing in its flight through three chaps but not badly wounding them. Of course there was a fine rumpus but it's very funny but they couldn't find the chap who fired it but expect they will in time. Well old chap how is the world using you? I suppose you are just knocking along the same as usual.
With best love to all, Yrs Pud.

Ray now enters the final part of his training , the next letter being the last from Colchester. His training is completed at Codford St. Mary in Wiltshire.

Hyderabad Barracks
Colchester
Dear Hal,
I am moving off on Monday and am marching to St. Albans and entraining to Salisbury. All the Colonels of our Brigade have just gone to France to receive orders for the Battalions so we shan't be long before we are on the way now. We are taking three days to march to St. Albans a distance of 65 miles. Our officers have had orders not to take any photos on the battlefield and some of them are very disappointed. Will write again later,
Yours Pud.

In May 1915 the 10th Essex, with the rest of the Division, bade farewell to Colchester after a strenuous but pleasant sojourn, having been ordered to Codford St. Mary, on Salisbury Plain. The march from Colchester was by way of Braintree, Bishop's Stortford and Hertford, at each of which places the night was spent. At Hertford train was taken to Codford, where the camp was large enough to accommodate the whole of the Division. The weeks rapidly passed in intensive training, which included trench digging at Yarnboro Castle, field training over Stony Hill, bombing, with missiles made out of jam pots, gas mask drill, with primitive cotton waste and black crepe, and Lewis gun classes.

Codford St Mary's
Wilts
Dear Hal,
Thanks muchly for your letter and the battery. I had a fairly good trip but it was too hot for marching and I began to think at one time that I should have to fall out but I managed to stick it. Yes! the 8th Norfolks are still with us, you see they can't take any of the Regts. out of the brigades now. There are four Regts. in our Brigade: 8th Norfolks, 10th Essex, 8th Suffolks, and 6th Royal Berks. and we are in the 53rd Brigade and the 18th Division. We were out all night so am having a rest today and are marching to Salisbury and back on Friday a distance of 26 miles. Hoping you are in the pink.
Yours Pud.

There are seven more letters during this period of training, all giving details of the work done. In his book "The 5th Army" Hubert Gough writes this of the training of the 18th Division by its Commander, Sir Ivor Maxse. "Although it was a new division, no division in the army was more efficiently trained from its commander, through its staff, down to the regimental officers and men.........." This was written after the outstanding success of the 18th Division on the first day of the Battle of the Somme, one of the few high points of that day.

A Coy.
10th Essex Regt.
No.3 Camp.
Codford St. Mary's.
Wilts.

Sunday 1915
Dear Hal,
Thanks very much for your last letter. I very nearly pegged out on that march, I got a bally blister the second day, and had a guard the first night so you can guess I wasn't fit for marching the next morning. We are absolutely in the Sahara Desert here, about 10 miles from anywhere. There are two shops in the village and one pub so you can guess what it is like for two divisions to be camped here. We are in huts and make our own electric light and have a pumping station for water, and you ought to see the hills we have to climb. We are 13 miles from Salisbury and 17 from Southampton, I was grousing about Colchester, but this place takes your breath away. Will write more later.
Yrs. Pud.

*Ray's notebook entries
from Lewis gun training*

16

Codford St. Mary's
Wilts.
Dear Hal,
Thanks ever so much for the baccy and letter. We had a great time with the artillery but some of the shrapnel nearly done in a platoon which got too far ahead but fortunately nobody was hurt. I have to do parades as well as look after the motor–cycles but I don't mind that as there is nothing else to do. Have just received the razor which I think is splendid. Our Colonel is now in the firing line, and if he isn't bowled over, we expect him back next week. We are firing our Trained Mans Course on Saturday and then we shall have finished all our firing. I should like to have seen them firing at the floating mine, I bet it was sport. Hope you are enjoying yourself on your bike and hope you are keeping in good health.
Yours ever, Pud.

The next three letters have the regimental crest embossed in gold in the top left hand corner.

Codford St Mary's
Wilts
Dear Hal,
Thanks awfully for the choc. which I enjoyed very much. We are getting now, 3 brigade days, and two divisional days a week with one days trenching, on brigade days we go 7 miles out then do an attack or defence, and on divisional days we go 12 miles out and do likewise. We rise now at 5a.m. and generally move off at 6–30a.m. and sometimes manage to get back at 5 p.m. Of course, now we have got our travelling kitchen its a lot better, because the grub is cooked while we are marching. We have found something to amuse us at last down here, some Belgium tarts have opened a tea–stall down here and they can only speak a few words of English, and I go down now and again with a pal and try some of my French on them, it isn't half a spree. I only wrote this letter so you could see what lovely paper I had captured. With love to all,
Yrs, Pud.

Ray's reference to "tarts" in this, and a later letter, is not meant in an insulting way, it simply meant 'girls'.

Pvt. Pudlo 17812
A Company
10th Essex Regt.
No3 Camp
Codford St. Mary's.
Wilts.
Dear Hal,
Thanks very much for your last letter. Yes! they are both brand new bikes the ones which I look after, and one is a 8 horse Indian and the other is a 3 and a half h.p. Triumph. Our C.C. had some very exciting times at the front, and since his address, we have had another from an Officer from the front, and he says that Kitcheners 1st and 2nd Armies

The photo taken "in town".

are to be the great striking force in this war, and that, when we get out there it will be one long bayonet charge. Am sending a Photo which I had done in town, You will notice the long bayonet which I swanked up to London in, I am sending some more later. Hoping you are fit. With love to all,
Yrs Pud

This is the first letter with any reference to Officers giving first hand reports from the front. As the time approaches for these newly trained volunteers to go to the front line, the greater the number of morale boosting talks.

Codford St Marys
Wilts
Saturday
Dear Hal,
Thanks ever so much for the baccy and also the Photo, shall I return it? Am afraid that our leave is off and we are doing that march next week and are doing 30 miles two days, and 15 the next making 75 miles. If that doesn't kill me, I don't know what will. Have got a weekend pass up to town this week. Yes! The roads are too bad about here to do over 40 miles an hr., but she can't half move. We had a big day last Thursday when the King inspected us at the Stonehenge, we had to walk nine miles to the ground, and I was only 5 yds off King Georgy when he came past. Then we had the march past which looked a treat and then we had three cheers for the King and at a given signal 20,000 men cheered and you can guess what it sounded like. With best love to all,
Yours Pud.

The regimental crested paper.

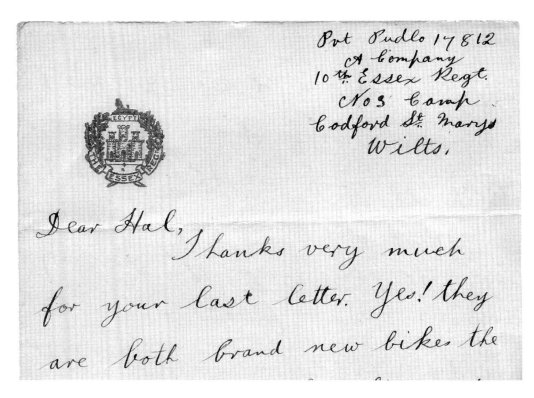

18

In July the Division was reviewed by H.M. the King near Stonehenge, and made a brave show as it marched past with bayonets glinting and fixed determination in every heart.

Before the 18th Division sailed the King sent a message of farewell: "Officers, Non–Commissioned Officers and men. You are about to join your comrades at the front in bringing to a successful end this relentless war of nearly twelve months duration. Your prompt patriotic answer to the Nation's call to arms will never be forgotten. The keen exertions of all ranks during the period of training have brought you to a state of efficiency not unworthy of my Regular Army. I am confident that on the field you will nobly uphold the traditions of the fine regiments whose names you bear. Ever since your enrolment I have closely watched the growth and steady progress of all units. I shall continue to follow with interest the fortunes of your Division. In bidding you farewell, I pray that God may bless you in all your undertakings."

Codford St Mary's
Wilts
Thursday
Dear Pa,
Thanks ever so much for the belt, it is just the thing. I have just returned from our three days march and feel absolutely done up, we slept two nights in open field and it was raining cats and dogs all the time, so you can guess we got pretty damp. Lord Kitchener didn't come down to Review us but King George came instead and he spoke very highly of the men and was sure that they would do credit to the country when we went out.... I am sending three more Photos for the family, they will have to fight it out between themselves as to who's to have them. Please excuse this scribble but the pen is slightly bent. With best love to all,
From your loving son, Raymond.

There is just one more letter from Codford St Mary's before Ray left for the front and it is particularly interesting as it contains a set of Battalion Orders for 15th July 1915. The orders reflect the imminent departure, only 10 days away.

Codford St Mary's
Wilts.
Dear Hal,
Thanks very much for your letter. The pork pie was a trifle gone but it went down alright. I was very wild to have missed May at Norwich but I couldn't get near the door as there were about 15 in the carriage. I should question very much if Theo knows where he is going anyway they don't give us any idear (sic). There is talk of us shifting next Thursday but nothing definite. I am sending you a copy of our orders I thought you might like to see. There were 72 chaps out of our Batt. overstayed their passes and have received, by doing so, 10 days Field Punishment and 12 days pay stopped and N.C.O.s have been stripped, there were 6 Lance–Corporals and 1 full. They are also to be the last to have leave when out at the front. You might tell them at home, to send the parcel as soon as pos., when it arrives.   With best love to all, Yrs. Pud.

BATTALION ORDERS BY
LIEUT. COLONEL B.O. FYFF   COMMANDING
IOTH (SERVICE) BATTALION   EX REGIMENT.
CODFORD ST.   RY.
T H U R S D A Y.   15TH. J   Y 1915.   ISSUE NO: 181.

P A R T   O N E.

I.   DETAIL.   Orderly Officer for the day - 2nd/Lieut. E.W. Bragg.

COMPANY FOR DUTY TOMORROW:-   "B" COMPANY.

PARADE TOMORROW:-   Bomb Throwing and Bayonet Fighting
by Companies Arrangements unless otherwise ordered.   *see below*

2.   MAPS, RETURN OF.   All maps that have been issued since the arrival
in this station are to be returned to the Orderly Room by IO a.m. tomorrow.

3.   BOMBERS ETC.   Officers Commanding Companies will render to the
Orderly Room by IO a.m. tomorrow, the No. of efficient Bombers, and the
No. of efficient Telephonists of their respective Companies.

4.   PORT OF EMBARKATION.   The following Brigade Order is republished
for information and compliance:-

" Information regarding Port of Embarkation, or names of Ships,
is to be regarded as secret, and not to be disclosed to anyone
except in the course of duty.   Officers and men are forbidden to
telegraph the above information to relations or friends when en route
to a port of embarkation ".

5.   FIRST AID DRESSINGS AND IODINE AMPOULES   Officers Commanding
Companies will ensure that all Officers, N.C.O's and men have first aid
dressings and iodine ampoules stitched to their tunics.
The first aid dressings will be obtained from the
Quarter-Master's Stores and the iodine ampoules from the Medical Officer.

6.   BOMB THROWING.   The following men having passed the required course
of bomb-throwing, are now entitled to wear their worsted grenades:-

        Pte. Wakefield......... "D" Coy
         "   Whitehead......... "D" "
         "   Sibley............ "D" "
         "   Juniper........... "D" "
         "   Wright R.J........ "D" "
         "   Clark E.H......... "D" "

7.   ROLLS TO BE RENDERED?   Officers Commanding Companies will forward to
Orderly Room by 9 a.m. on Sunday the 18th instant, alphabetical rolls in
duplicate of all N.C.O's and men inoculated against Enteric Fever.
These rolls should show the number of times inoculated and also
the dates on which the inoculations were given.
A record of inoculations is to be made on the top of the inside
of the right hand cover of Army Book 64 (Soldiers' Pay Book), as follows:-
T.V.2 or T.V.1 with the initials of the medical Officer, and the
date or dates on which the inoculations were given.
T.V.2 will indicate that the "two doses" system has been
followed, and T.V.1 that the individual has had only one dose of C.CM. of
Typhoid Vacine.

8.   INSURANCE CARDS.   Reference Battalion Orders No: 3 of the 6th
instant.   Certificates should be sent to the Orderly Room at once
certifying that all Cards have been stamped and issued for half-year
ending July 3rd. 1915.
The new cards should be in readiness for dis-
posal immediately on receipt of Embarkation Orders, under Company
arrangements vide Mob. Reg: para: 192 (a).

20

FROM THE FRONT

At midnight on July 25th 1915 Ray sailed with his regiment from Folkestone to Boulogne, arriving at 3 a.m. on 26th July.

In the evening of the 26th July the Battalion entrained for Bertangles, lying N.W. of Amiens, and arrived at a siding about a mile distant from the village as dawn was breaking. Thence the Battalion marched eight miles to Rubempre through peaceful country, rich with the devastation of war.... At Rubempre the transport and machine guns rejoined. The Essex men were the first British troops billeted in the village and they were not impressed with the amenities.... After inspection by the Corps. commander in a thunderstorm on August 2nd in a field near the chateau at Molliens–au–Bois, the 10th Essex and 6th Royal Berkshire marched 12miles to Bouzincourt.

> **The Essex Regiment**
> **10th Battalion**

The men of the 10th Essex went to the sector of trenches held by the 152nd Infantry Brigade of the 51st (Highland Division). The men went into the trenches, 2 companies at a time, for 48 hours under instruction. Each rank was attached to a similar rank and

A final picture card to his mother from Folkestone.

21

The trench map for the Thiepval area for this period from the 10th Essex War Diary. To see these trench maps in location, see the 'Support and Resource' unit for this book at www.poppyland.co.uk.

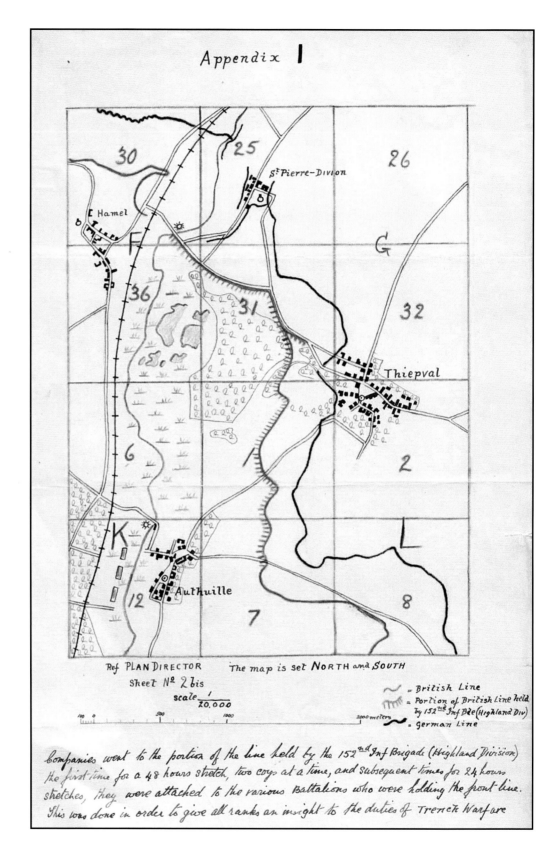

Appendix I

Companies went to the portion of the line held by the 152nd Inf Brigade (Highland Division) the first time for a 48 hours stretch, two coys at a time, and subsequent times for 24 hours stretches, they were attached to the various Battalions who were holding the front line. This was done in order to give all ranks an insight to the duties of Trench Warfare duty as the Highland Division thus obtaining first–hand insight into trench warfare. This period of instruction took place between August 6th and August 12th 1915. The area of trenches, which gave Ray his first taste of the front line, was near the villages of Authuille and Thiepval, names which were destined to become synonymous with bitter fighting and heavy British losses a year later. For now it was a relatively quiet sector, perhaps not too severe an introduction to trench warfare.

We have three letters from this time, two before Ray went into the trenches.

Pvt. R.Randall 17812
A Coy 10th Essex (SB)Batt.
53rd Inf.Brigade
18th Division,
B.E.F.
Dear Ma and Dad,
I am somewhere in France but am not at liberty to give any details. We had a quiet crossing and am getting quite fat on dog biscuit and bully beef. I had thought of sending some cash home, but as this passes through the hands of the censor, I think it advisable not to. The weather has been fairly good but have had a little rain. Some of our transport men say they have heard the guns, but I haven't heard them myself yet. Hoping you are all well at home as this leaves me the same.
From your loving son, Raymond.

17812 No 1 Platoon
A Coy 10th Essex (SB) Reg, 53rd Inf. Brigade
18th Division
B.E.F. Sunday
Dear Pater and Ma,
Thanks very much for the parcels and contents also for the welcome letters, which have just received. Did you get my other letter? I find the French phrase book very useful and am just beginning to get acquainted with the language. We have been practising bayonet fighting and done two short marches since we have been down here. We have to take our rifles with us where–ever we go, even when we go for a walk, and always have five rounds in the magazine.
....................Is Theo gone to Egypt yet? You might let me have his address. We are getting paid out in French money and have just received a 5 franc note. Have no more to write just now. With best love to all,
From your loving son, Raymond.

Thursday Aug12th
1915
Dear Pa & Ma,
I have just received your letters and "Cromer Post" for which many thanks. I am sorry to say I have lost my lighter. I am glad you have received some of my letters. I expect you will have had some more by the time this reaches you. I had some narrow escapes

Brother Theo was a member of the 5th Norfolks, a territorial battalion. He would serve with them in Gallipoli.

last night in the trenches from the German shells which were bursting all around, it was mostly shrapnel but haven't any coal–boxes yet. I haven't lost the pipe Hal presented me with yet, but it's surprising the amount of cigarettes that are smoked in the trenches. I haven't used all the Pomade yet, the tin is still three–quarters full. I have found the periscope invaluable for trench work, and I believe it has saved my life several times. .... We have had no signs of gas on our front, they say the Germans haven't used it where we are, and I hope they won't. ....The only rotten job in the trenches is fetching the grub, we have to travel about 2 miles of communication trenches over which the enemy every now and then drop a shell on the off chance of catching someone. I think this is all just now with best love to all.
From your loving son, Raymond.

A philosophical view of this period is given in this contemporary account.

**The Essex Regiment
10th Battalion**

We, one and all, went into the line quite prepared to do or die. There was quite a whisper one of the afternoons as we took over that an attack was to be made at dawn. This, of course, was only a rumour. What we should have done had we been ordered to scale our own parapets at a moments notice, but few had wondered. Those four days instruction were invaluable to us. They got our perspective right and enabled us to commence thinking in terms of the possible. Doubtless we had been very serious in our training in England, but we had thought of, and often acted, the impossible. We left oppressive seriousness and unbalanced plans buried deep in the trenches at Thiepval.

At 3 p.m. on August 13th the Battalion marched to Vecquemont on the outskirts of Daours on the river Somme. They arrived at their billets at 9–15 p.m. The chief employment while at Daours was platoon and company training.

**The Essex Regiment
10th Battalion**

The nine days spent in Daours were amongst the happiest in France and eighteen months later we were still censoring letters to members of the fair sex, both young and old, of that town. On August 20th the 53rd Brigade, less the 8th Norfolks, were inspected by M. Millerand, the French Minister of War.

17812 B.E.F.
Aug. 15th 1915
Dear Hal,
Thanks ever so much for your letter. I think I have received all the parcels safely so far, I have received three up to now. We have certain days for washing but of course you can't get all the dirt out with cold water, still we make them [uniforms] somewhat presentable. I should say there was a fault in the magneto of Clementines when it was new and it has gradually developed.* Yes! Wilf wrote and told me he was down at the docks and says he is quite enjoying it. I hope Reg gets his commission. I think he would look a treat in a kilted regiment. It all seems like a dream being out here in fact I don't realise I am in a foreign country. I don't think I've any more news just now.
With best love to all, Yours ever, Pud

* *Clementine was a motor bike.*

17812
A Coy No 1 Platoon
10th Essex Regt.
B.E.F.
Tuesday 17th Aug
Dear Pa and Ma, Please note the change of address, no Brigade or Division must be put on the letter or parcels now, because it causes confusion at the sorting office. Thanks very much Ma for the respirator, but I hope I shall never need it. ....We are now preparing for an inspection by the French Minister which comes off on Friday, then we are to be shifted to an even warmer climate than the one we have just come from. ....

Wednesday Aug. 15th.
Dear Pa, have just received your letter dated Aug. 15th...................... Ma says she has lost the list of my comrades so I am repeating them. ....
We have just got a machine for throwing bombs to be used in the trenches and it will throw them about 250 yds. and one bomb will kill everyone in the traverse. They have

a funny way of punishing the chaps in the R.F.A.* out here, they strap them to the gun–wheels for so many hours every day. I think this is all just now, With best love to all, From your loving son, Raymond P.S. The names of my comrades are as follows: Pvt. O. Fletcher 14877, Pvt. A. Wheeler 15401 Pvt. J.E. Robinson 17807.

*Royal Field Artillery

22–8–15 11a.m. March to Bray. Arr. 9p.m. (2 halts of 2 hrs.). Billets found to be dirty.
23–8–15 to 27–8–15 Brigade Reserve in billets.

The 53rd Brigade, now that the initiatory trench training had been completed, had become responsible for a sector of the line. It was to take over from the Carnoy–Mametz road (exclusive) to a small quarry, known as the "D–Francais" sector. The 8th Suffolks and 6th Royal Berkshire were the first

Brothers Wilf and Reg - who did indeed obtain his commission.

10th Essex War Diary

With the 10th Essex in France

Comrades

to take charge of the trenches whilst the 10th Essex and 8th Norfolks were in reserve. When waiting for their turn these units constructed a series of bomb–proof shelters in Happy Valley about one and a half miles north of Bray, whilst a company was also employed in duplicating the existing trenches from the Citadel to Wellington Redoubt and in finding working parties for a mining section in the front line. When engaged upon the latter the Germans exploded a mine which injured six men, though not seriously.

It was not until the night of the 5th September that the 10th Essex relieved the 6th Royal Berkshires. There are three letters written before this date. The first is postmarked 26th Aug 1915. The other two are undated but are around this time.

Letter postmarked 26th Aug 1915
17812
Dear Hal, Thanks very much for your letter. My parcels take about 5 days to get through and the letters vary from two days to five. Thanks ever so much for the lighters the simpler type is the best and most effective. It's hard luck about old 'Clementine' but expect you will have to grin and bear it. Have got down to the firing line again after a little rest at the base but have got to a new position about 10 miles further up the line. How is Reg getting on? Has he got his commission yet? The Zepps. have been pretty busy on the East Coast haven't they, do you know which part they visited? I haven't time for any more just now so will close.
With love to all, Yrs ever, Pud.

17812
A Coy.No1 Platoon
10th Essex Regt.
B.E.F.
Dear Pa & Ma,
Thanks very much for the last batch of letters dated Aug.22nd 1915.... Dear Ma, Am sending a post–card I purchased here and it was worked by the French girls so I thought you would like it. ....We are supplied with clean things at the base and have a bath at the same time. I haven't been troubled with insects yet, but there are plenty of rats in the trenches.... While I am writing this letter the guns are banging away continually and a few odd shells come over now and again. We are now lying

in support and take our turn in the fire trenches later, that is if we are not shelled out before. Shall have to close now as I have to go on fatigue.
With best love to all, From your loving, Raymond.

17812
Dear Pa & Ma,
I have received your letter dated Aug.26th for which many thanks. Am afraid the delays in letters can't be remedied.... We had a few casualties the other night in our company when the Germans blew up one of their mines and a few of our chaps got wounded. This is a very warm shop where we are now and the mines which are blown up on either side, every night or two, make an awful mess of the trenches and anybody who happens to

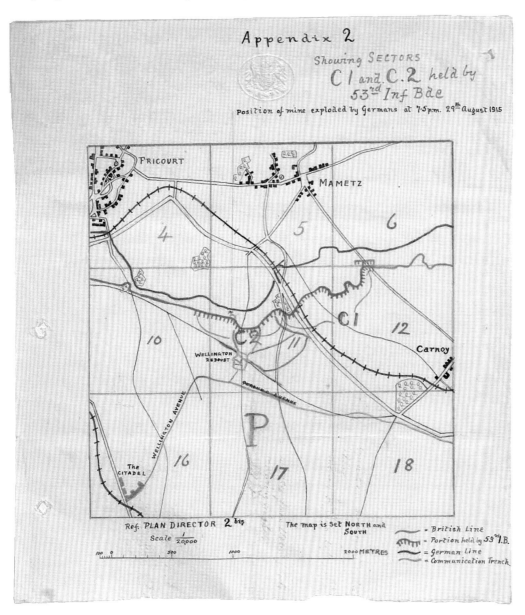

The 10th Essex War Diary map records where the enemy mine was exploded on 29th August 1915.

be in them. At the time of writing have just come back from a mining expedition, these mines or saps generally have a shaft like a coal—pit which goes down about 40ft then goes along under the German trenches, when you are nearing the German trenches you can sometimes hear them making another sap and of course there is plenty of chances of them blowing you up before you have finished the sap. Please let me have a list of the casualties of the 5th Norfolks if you can get them. Am at present still keeping well and fit and you and Ma are doing the same.
With best love to all,
From your loving son, Raymond.

10th Essex War Diary

5–9–15 Battalion moved by companies to relieve 6th R.Berks. under cover of darkness. Trenches 70–75(inc.) sector C2 taken over. Last company completed relief 2–30a.m. 6th Sept. 'A' Company in reserve in Wellington Redoubt.('A' Company came in from Citadel.) Enemy fired about 60 grenades, enemy's sniper active opposite points 73 & 74. No damage done. On average enemy trenches 180yds away except where Saps and extensions at point 'D' converge here about 45 yds. Enemies flares appear to be superior to ours.
7–9–15 3–30a.m. Battalion stood to arms. Enemy snipers active and accurate. R.F.A. fired 8 rounds Shrapnel. Enemy fired 7 high explosive shells into Wellington Redoubt 10–40a.m.

Ray's next letter appears to reflect the above activity.

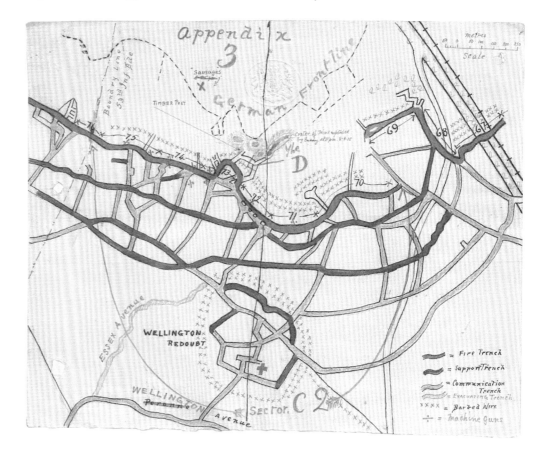

A detailed map of Wellington Redoubt and the trenches in the vicinity, from the 10th Essex War Diary. As with other maps in the book, it can be seen in context by visiting the "Support and Resource" pages associated with this book at www.poppyland.co.uk.

17812

Thursday 9th Sept.

Dear Pa & Ma, Have just received your letter for which many thanks.... The Germans blew up another mine last night but am glad to say no severe casualities (sic) occurred, they also sent over a few pills in way of shells which also did no serious damage. I expect to shift from the reserve to the firing line on Sunday and from what I have seen of it, will have a warm time. It's very difficult to get a wash up here in the trenches, because of the awkwardness of getting it (water) up, I have had two this week. I don't know whether we shall ever make an advance here, it isn't safe to put your little finger over the trench in the daytime. I wish Theo had come out here, he would have been a lot better off.... Am sorry to hear Reg's efforts have failed, but tell him to stick to it. With best love to all, From your loving son, Raymond.

13–9–15 3–30p.m. Relief of Companies. 'A' company relieved 'C' company (trenches 70–72)

7–30p.m. Battalion stood to arms
11–15p.m. 3 "sausages" reported to have come over from usual direction i.e. point 311. Howitzers informed and fired 2 rounds at that point.

Ray often mentions "sausages" .They were fearsome missiles, usually consisting of a metal drum 2ft long and 1ft in diameter, with a handle at each end. The casing was thin and the cylinder contained about 50lbs of high explosive. They tended to rotate end over end in flight.

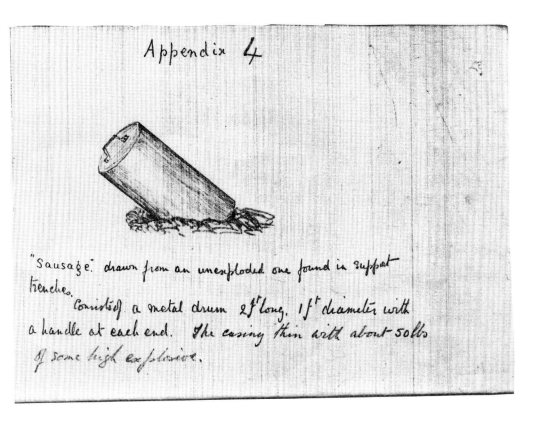

The "sausage" was a sufficiently new development at that time to warrant this sketch in the 10th Essex War Diary.

16–9–15 3–30a.m. Stood to arms – all quiet.
6–15p.m.to 6–45p.m. Enemy bombed and shelled support trenches,72–75 considerably.
7p.m. Firing died down and bombing ceased.
7–45p.m. 1st Norfolks relieved. Completed 2–15a.m. 17th Sept. via Wellington Ave. Returned to billets at Bray until 7a.m. when Battalion moved to Morlancourt by companies at 5 minute intervals arriving 8p.m.–8–30p.m."
18–9–15 6–45p.m. Marched Buire 1/4hr. intervals into billets in Divisional Reserve.

Ray wrote to his "Pa & Ma" on the 17th September; to Harold on the 18th Septembr..

17812 Sept.17th 1915.
Dear Pa & Ma, Thanks very much for the last letter dated 12th. This makes my third week in the trenches and I shan't be sorry when I get out and have a wash. I read the piece in the "Post" about Theo and am glad he is still alright. Am sorry to say, have lost one of my comrades today, he was killed by a sniper, and hit by an explosive bullet in the head. We had a little scrap with the Germans the other night, for a crater left by the explosion of a mine and for about half–an–hour it was very lively, but we captured the crater all right. I manage to boil about 6 pints of water with the tinned heat, which I don't think is at all bad.... I expect to be coming out for a fortnights rest in a day or two, which we are very much in need of. I think this is all just now. With best wishes to all, From your loving son, Raymond. xxxxxxxxxxx

Above is Buire in a card sent by Ray. Below is a photograph of Buire in 2007.

17812 Sept.18th 1915
Dear Hal, Have just received parcel all serene for which many thanks and also many thanks for your letter. I am now out of the trenches for a rest after having been in them three weeks. Yes! It was quite easy to use grenades on the enemy's trenches and of course they could do likewise to ours. I am glad those 'Zepps' didn't go near Brockley or Penge I hear they did plenty of damage this time. Thanks very much for the refill, I find the pocket lamp invaluable. I manage to boil about 6 pints of water with the tinned heat which I don't think is at all bad. Please thank Mr Wills ever so much for the "cigars" you ought to see how the other chaps envy me. The first Norfolks relieved us out of the trenches or what was left of them. The periscope is still in working order, but have had one or two narrow shaves of it being broken, I had to disguise it in the end with a sandbag. Am glad to hear 'Clementine' is still going strong and pleased to hear you have had such good luck with the tyres. The snipers out here use explosive bullets and they don't half make a gash if they hit you, am sorry to say one of my pals got hit by one, but am

not quite sure whether he is dead yet. Aeroplanes are so common that I hardly notice them now, and I've seen the Germans fire as many as 70 shells at one British plane over their lines and then not bring it down. I suppose there is a Aerodrome on Mousehold?* I think this is all just now ,
With best love, Yrs. ever, Pud.

* Mousehold Heath, Norwich

By the time the 1st Norfolks relieved the 10th Essex, as mentioned in Ray's diary and letter, they were relative veterans of the war. The 1st & 2nd Battalions of the Norfolks were two regular army regiments at the outbreak of World War One. The 1st Norfolks were part of the original "Contemptibles" and had fought with the 15th Infantry Brigade at the Battle of Mons. They then spent many weeks trench bound in the waterlogged misery of the Ypres Salient, in the vicinity of the notorious Hill 60. The casualty list for 4 days in March tells its own story: March 3rd 1915; one officer and 6 men killed, 19 men wounded, March 17th and 18th; one officer and 11 men killed, one officer and 46 men wounded, March 20th; 7 men killed, 2 officers and 31 men wounded.

In May 1915 they also became victims of the deadly gas attacks. On May 5th there were 75 Battalion casualties as a result of gas.

For the 1st Norfolks a move to the relatively quiet sector of the Somme in September must have been almost a pleasure. Mention of the Somme at this stage of the war did not evoke any particular feeling of dread, it was just another river in France.

The 10th Essex remained in Divisional reserve at Buire until the 26th September and was, with the 7th East Kents, inspected by Lord Kitchener on 21st. The ceremony took place in a field just south of the Albert–Amiens road near Ribemont.

17812 Sept.24th 1915
Dear Pa, Thanks very much for your letter. ....I am sorry to say my watch has gone out of action, I can hardly wonder at it myself because it has had some severe shakings. We are going into the trenches again in a day or two and the way we have been working it so far, will mean 3 weeks in and one out. ....Thanks very much for the water sterilisers they will be most useful later on. I should think they have some very low standards in the 6th Norfolks to take a little shrimp like Sidney Kirby. I think this is all just now.
With best love from your loving son, Raymond.

P.S. Could manage one of those tinned heats every week if possible.

26–9–15 2p.m. Battalion marched to trenches via ALBERT. Companies marched at ½ hour intervals to relieve the 8th Suffolks. Relief complete.
9–30p.m. Distribution of Battalion, 'C' Coy. on right front line(120–121) 'B' Coy. on centre front line (122–124) 'D' Coy. on left front line (124–126). 'A' Coy. in Reserve. Coys. relieve each other every 48 hours."

| 10th Essex War Diary |

8–57p.m. Trench mortars fired from opposite "ILOT". 12 midnight 6 "Whiz–Bangs" (enemy's light field gun) fired at support trenches of 122–123 between 10 p.m. and 2 a.m.

As the map below shows, the Battalion was in a sector of trenches at La Boisselle, a small village about three miles from the town of Albert on the Bapaume road. Ray was to spend the next five months in and out of trenches in this area. At La Boisselle the British and German trenches were closer than anywhere else on the whole of the Western Front. The following entry from the War Diary is typical of this period.

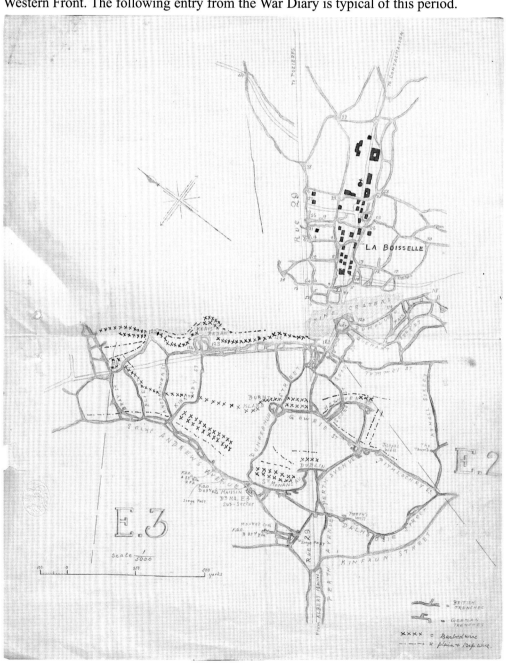

27–9–15 3–45a.m. Battalion stood to arms. All quiet. 6–00a.m. Small mine exploded by our engineers opposite T sap. Miners reported that one enemy Machine Gun and one sniper's listening post were destroyed.

All quiet until 2p.m. from which time onwards till midnight at intervals the enemy fired 28 heavy trench mortars and 15 rifle grenades from the trenches on West of La Boisselle over to our trenches in rear of "ILOT". They were answered by six 4.5inch Howitzers. Enemy working party in left crater opposite ILOT. We bombed them and work stopped. 6–15p.m. 2nd Lt. Hudson shot through brain, died instantaneously. 6–45p.m. Stood to arms.

10th Essex War Diary

The chief interest for the 10th Essex in this sector was the Western part of the village street, which jutted out from the remainder of the line and was known as the "ILOT". It was a queer conglomeration of shallow, narrow slits between old and new sandbags, foundations of and rubble from destroyed houses, a cemetery and used and disused mine shafts. These served for trenches.

The Essex Regiment
10th Battalion

The first letter we have from Ray at this time is to his Father dated Sept. 30th. It is preceded with an entry from the War Diary.

29–9–15 5–55p.m. 12 enemy mortars did considerable amount of damage to parapet and to 2 dug–outs in the trenches behind the Ilot. Buried 17 men, 4 of whom were killed and 13 injured.

These casualties were in Ray's company.

17812 Sept.30th 1915.
Dear Pa,
Thanks ever so much for your letter which have just received. I see by your letter that Theo has had another lucky escape and am glad he got off so lightly. I am now in a new part of the line and the Germans are very hot at trench mortars in this part. We have just had another casualty list in our Coy. A German trench mortar burst on one of the dug–outs and buried several of our fellows and am sorry to say some of them have been killed. We are very close to the Germans here, and in one place the two trenches nearly touch each other, so it is impossible to use rifle fire, but there's plenty of bombs buzzing about. I saw Russell Hunt and Young Saddler about a week ago, the 8th Norfolks are next to us on the line. Did you receive my last letter, I mentioned that my watch was out of action in it, I wondered if you could let me have another one as I felt lost without it.
With best love, from your loving son, Raymond.

The cemetery at La Boisselle during the conflict and in 2007.

This letter was written in the trenches and is the start of another personal saga, this time with regard to watches! The "village" mentioned in the letter is La Boisselle.

17812 Oct.3rd 1915
Dear Hal, Thanks awfully for the watch, and letter, do you know that was just the kind of watch I wanted, because it's rather dangerous showing a light in the trenches at

night. I expect you have seen by the papers that things are getting lively out here. In this new part of the line where I am now the Germans have got an awful lot of sausage guns and they send them over by the dozen. Yes! The snipers are always trying to break the glass of my periscope but they haven't succeeded yet. The part where I am in now runs through what was once the street of a village of course the houses are nowhere to be seen, but there is half a lamp post on the side of the trench and a crucifix which strange to say hasn't been touched yet. Am glad to hear you have got the bike running again and think you will find that the pull will improve as it gets running again. Yes! I think it adds to the interest if you have a speedometer on, you can tell just what she will do, if it came to a push. Please thank Mr. Wills for the choc. which have just received and also Reg for the cigs. and everybody for their contributions in the parcel. In one part of our trench the two parapets nearly touch in fact the German trench is only 10 yds. away, there is no rifle fire at this point as you can guess but a chap stands there with bombs and every now and then chucks one and the Germans do likewise. We had our first frost the other night and I stood at the parapet watching it come on and gradually freezing at the same time. Some of our chaps heard the Germans shout across the other night, "When are you blighters going to stand to?" in fairly good English. I think this is all just now. With best love to all, Yours ever, Pud.

7–10–15 Relieved by 1st Coy. 8th Suffolks between 10–30a.m. and 12–30p.m. Battalion in billets at Albert in Brigade reserve. Billets in Albert good and compact. Good place for transport.

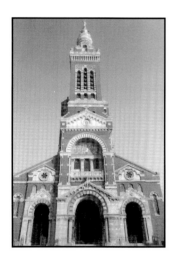

The Basilica in Albert was greatly damaged during the war but post-war was fully restored.

The chief buildings of Albert, including the cathedral, had been sadly knocked about by the German fire prior to the British Army taking over this portion of the line from the French. The greater part of the town was intact however . Only a few hundreds of inhabitants remained and there was ample accommodation for the Battalion. Many estaminets remained open, whilst the town baths enabled every man to have a wash and change of clothes. Digging in the Albert defences, which were paved with bricks from the ruined houses, and instruction in the system of supporting artillery fire provided serious occupation and football and cinema entertainments were the lighter relief.

17812 Oct.8th 1915
Dear Ma & Pa, Thanks ever so much for your last letter. I have been having a fairly lively time, but have not taken part in the big advance. Our part of the line hasn't made a move yet, but I don't think we shall be long now. The Germans have invented a new shell now to deal with respirators it's called the Tear shell and it rips the respirator so the gas can penetrate.... My comrades are all serene, bar the one I told you about. In reference to the explosive bullet, I mean the small shell, the German snipers use a lot of them. The watch Hal sent is splendid and will be most useful in the trenches. Young Sidney Kirby must have sprouted since I last saw him. I expect by the time you receive this letter that I shall be out of the trenches for a short rest after being in them ten days this time. I think this is all just now.
With best love to all, From your loving son, Raymond. xxxxxxxxx

Above, Albert 2007. Below, left, are two First World War photographs as 'before and after' views.

28 — ALBERT (Somme) - La Place d'Armes

Life when out of the trenches was far from complete rest, particularly if you were still close to the front line. The following, from the War Diary, gives an idea of life in Albert.

8–10–15 In Billets as Brigade reserve–cleaning equipment. 9–10–15 In Billets as Brigade reserve. One company digging on Albert defences at the extreme Easterly end of Albert to South of Bapaume Road (Rue 29) under supervision of Sussex Pioneer Officers.

Numerous fatigues such as carrying Royal Engineers stores for tunnelling companies, physical exercises and handling of arms. Party of 400 sent to bath at Brigade Baths during the day. Concert in cinema hall in the evening.

10th Essex War Diary

Guerre 1914-1915
96 — ALBERT (Somme) - La Place d'Armes après le bombardement.

Ray expands on this way of life in the following letters.

17812 [postmarked Oct.11th.]
Dear Hal, I am just writing to ask you to send another watch like the last one as my

section Sergt. has taken a fancy to mine and asked me to get him one like it. I will forward later three five franc notes which I think will cover the cost of postage and what you will lose in changing the notes. I think this is all just now.
With best love, Yrs. Pud.

The next letter is undated but refers to the period just after the Battalion had taken billets in Albert. The "notes" referred to are payment for watches.

17812 Dear Hal,
Thanks ever so much for your letter and please thank everyone for their contributions to the parcel. You might let me know when you get the notes I sent. I had a very funny surprise the other day when I was out, I went into a shop, (or rather what was once a shop), and started rattling off my best French to the "tart" who served, but was stopped in the middle of my speech by the calm enquiry as to whether it wouldn't be better for me to start over again in English, well I was struck all of a heap. In this town where I am now billeted we are only about a mile and a half from the firing line so it is nice and handy for the trenches. We are using a picture–palace for a concert hall and our band gives selections and it is very strange how this palace escaped getting hit when this place was under shellfire. We get a shell over now and again when we are having a concert but that doesn't interfere with the singing. By the way could you send me something for the toothache I get every now and again. Our General said that if we make this our base, that he would rig the picture palace up again and get some new films, so I hope we do. I hear we start leave when we come out of the trenches next time but as to the arranging of it, I'm not quite sure about it. I am enclosing a few cards, please give one of coloured ones to Syb, and the rest you can do what you like with. I expect I shall be in the trenches again by the time you get this. Please excuse the writing, mistakes etc., as I am writing this by a rotten French candle. Yes! We use trench mortars , but ours are not half as bad as theirs. Yes! I throw a bomb over to the Germans now and again but I always get one back so I don't throw more than I can help you bet. I shall have to have a good look round 'Clementine' when I come home and see if I can't trickulate her up. I think those 'snaps' you sent were splendid. I see Reg is still a 'lad', and I think that is an angelic smile of yours. Please thank Mr Wills for the choc. One lighter has given up the ghost but the other is still in service (the simple one). Thanks muchly for the matches they are very useful after using these things the French call matches. They have just dished us out with a blanket so have got about another twenty pounds to carry up to the trenches. Please thank Reg for the 'Horlicks' which needless to say I enjoy very much and am not in need of extra clothes yet but will write if I am. With best love to all, Yours ever, Pud.

17812 Oct. 14th 15
Dear Pa,
Thanks very much for your letter
which I have just received. .... We have now a Divisional Cinema Palace working, about three or four miles from our billets and some of us were taken to the opening of it, in motor buses. I find it very difficult to write, because nothing exciting has happened out here worth speaking of. I thought Con. Moulton was for home service, anyway I

wish him luck if he's coming out here. .... Do you know whether Tommy Parker went out with the Yeomanry? I am glad to say I am in the best of health and have never felt fitter. We had a service for Wes. in our Picture Palace last Sunday and our Chaplain gave us a very enjoyable evening. I'm afraid Reg. has gone in for some hard graft by joining a horse Regt. but all the same wish him the best of luck. One of my comrades has joined our mining section of the R.E.s and has I believe gone home on leave his name is Walker and lives at Sporle near Swaffham. I think this is all just now.
With best love to all, Your loving Son, Raymond.

On 15th October 1915 it was back to the trenches to relieve the 8th Suffolks. The War Diary reports that Companies moved up at half hour intervals to E3 sub sector. The relief was completed at 12–30p.m.

4–45p.m. 3 "sausages" behind Ilot one pitched in Scone Street doing damage to trench and burying 3 men (one killed, 2 injured). 16–10–15 4–35p.m. Germans exploded a small mine on North side of Ilot damaged our S2 and H shafts and blew about 20yds of left (N) face of Ilot, buried 3 men in S2.

10th Essex War Diary

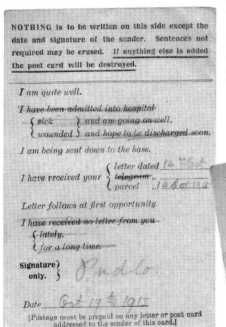

Ray sent a Field Service Postcard on October 19th, perhaps thinking he wouldn't have time for a letter. However he did write a letter on the 19th from the trenches. Both the above War Diary entries are referred to in the letter.

17812 Oct.19th 15
Dear Hal,
Have received your letter and watch also have received this weeks parcel and last weeks, I thought I had told some of the people at home about it. Will you be able to change the notes all right? I'm sorry to trouble you again, but could you send another

watch as I have another customer, in one of our Corperals (sic). You didn't let me know whether I sent enough cash. I hear the Zepps. were over Croyden and there was a big casualty list. I also received the flash lamp bulb for which many thanks. My pal Wheeler had a lucky escape the other day, he was walking up the communication trench behind me, when a grenade burst on our right,

Albert Wheeler

and I turned round when I heard the clatter of his rifle in the trench and saw him gently reposing in the bottom, a piece of the grenade had struck him on the head, but fortunately it was nearly spent and only inflicted a small wound, from which I am glad to say he is quite recovered. I am sorry to say we started our casualty list directly we got into the trenches this time, a "sausage" burst right on the edge of the trench, bringing down about a ton of earth and burying three of our fellows, two of whom got out alive but the third was dead. The Germans also blew up one of their mines and buried some of the miners who were down one of ours. Will forward the notes when I come out of the trenches again. Please thank everybody for their contributions to the parcel and tell them I am writing later as I don't get a lot of time in the trenches. Am glad those old Zeps. didn't drop any bombs when they passed over Cromer. I am still alive and kicking and feel fit for anything, hoping you are the same. With best love to all,
Yrs. ever, Pud.

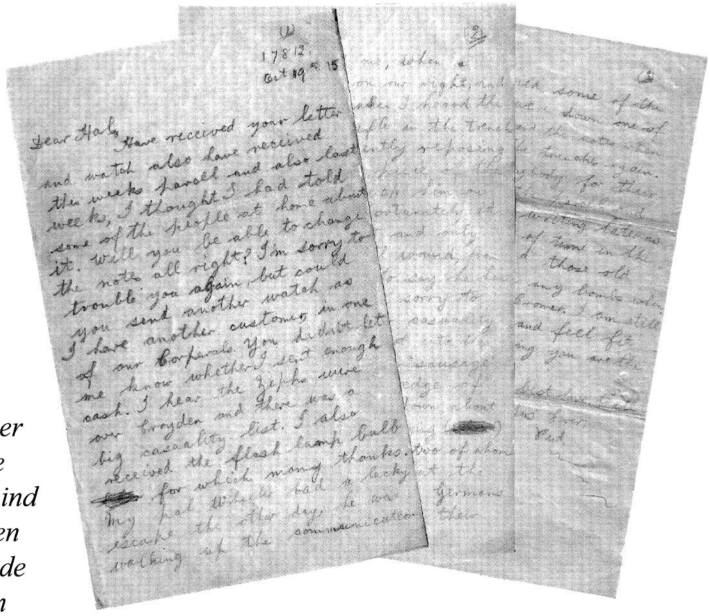

In this letter Ray mentions his pal "Wheeler". This was Albert Wheeler of Colchester who was well known in the Battalion for his "comic turns" at concert parties.

With the 10th Essex in France

Those evenings are worth recalling. We had a fair amount of talent in the Battalion; the Divisional troops stationed in the town provided the rest. Private Wheeler, of "A" Company, was our star; we revelled in him. Like the rest of our artists, he delighted in appearing in quaint civilian attire rescued from attics and lumber rooms of various billets. He had a merry, funny face, and was never at a loss for an apt retort, or joke, on

38

any recent trench incident. His turn which I best remember commenced in a boisterous manner with the couplet:–

> "'Twas Christmas Day in the workhouse,"

and after a serious pause,

> "'Twas Christmas Day outside as well!"

A little later we were told that at the workhouse Christmas dinner one of the inmates was indiscreet enough to say in a loud voice,"curse the carrots, give me turnips". Wheeler was ever ready to lend a hand to one of his less talented comrades, and one night he turned the maiden effort of another man, which had about reached the "rude remark stage, into a howling success. Wheeler appeared suddenly from behind the scenes as a lunatic one–arm boxer; the audience was immediately in good humour, and the turn lasted some 15 minutes. Wheeler was killed in the Delville Wood fighting of 1916, and we were greatly poorer for the loss of his gaiety. He was one of the best known characters in the original Battalion.

He was killed on 20th July 1916, ironically the day after Ray was wounded and still lying in Delville Wood. Albert Wheeler's grave was never found and his name appears on the Thiepval Memorial to the missing on the Somme along with over 70,000 other names.

The Battalion were relieved on the 23rd of October. The day before, Ray wrote a graphic letter to his father.

17812   Oct.22nd 1915
Dear Pa,
Thanks ever so much for your letter. I have just written to Harold, and asked him to send out another watch, and now our Capt. has asked me to get him a wrist watch with luminous dial for preference, or one like the last one sent if you can't get a wrist watch, he wants a fairly cheap one. Have just had 48 hrs. in one of the hottest parts of our line and have had a lively time. In no part of the corner, (where we were on sentry duty), were we less than 20 yds from the Germans and in one place we were only 7 yds from them. There was plenty of work for the bombers and we got rid of about 200 and received back about twice as many besides one or two sausages but am glad to say have had only one killed and several wounded. You see some funny sights in the trenches at night, the other night a big white cat ran along the parapet, it gave me quite a start for a minute or two, but he buzzed off too quick for me to have a pop at him. Had a narrow escape from a sausage, it bounced on the parapet in front of me, then bounced onto the parapet behind, it was only the difference of a couple of feet as to whether it would alight in the trench and I shouldn't have been writing this letter now if it had. Yes! I received the bulb you sent some time ago but I gave it to an R.E. in the trenches who was in a fix with his lamp as he had to go down a mine. I could do with a writing pad once a fortnight and a battery once in three weeks now the nights are longer. The Germans here are pretty nervous they keep thinking we are going to attack, and sweep our parapets every day with machine–gun fire and also send rifle grenades over by the dozen. Mabs wrote and told me about the Zeps. it must have been exciting.
With best love to all,
from your loving son, Raymond.

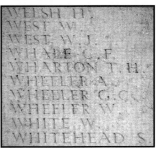

The monument at Thiepval and Albert Wheeler's name on the memorial.

His sister Mabel (Mabs) was teaching in south London, so presumably had seen the 'Zeps' (Zeppelins) there.

23–10–15 Battalion relieved by 8th Suffolk Regiment. Marched to Battalion reserve at Buire.

On this day Ray sent a letter to another of his brothers, Reg.

17812 Oct.23rd 15
Dear Reg,
Thanks very much for your letter, I am glad to hear you have a decent billet and hope you are enjoying yourself cleaning harness. Have just finished 8 days in the trenches, and also in a hot place, one spot in particular we were only 9 yds. from the Germans it has been nick–named "Hell's Corner" and what with hand grenades and sausages it has been a very unhealthy spot. I suppose you haven't a regiment number yet? I see they get you on the button cleaning dodge, do they come round with a pair of field–glasses and examine your chin to see if you have shaved? They used to with us, when we were in training. We have had very decent weather in the trenches this time...................... Well shall have to close now as I have to go on mining fatigue, but am not like Daddy because I do go down the mine.
With best love, Yrs., Pud.
P.S. Take a tip from an old soldier the less you do in the Army the more they think of you.

Buire, 24–10–15. Practice ceremonial parade for inspection by H.M. THE KING.
25–10–15. H.M. The King inspected 2 battalions from each Division in 10th Corps of which this Btn. [10thEssex] was one.

.... On 25th October battalions from the 5th, 51st and 18th Divisions paraded under command of General Maxse, one mile north of Ribecourt, and were inspected by the King and President Poincare. The Prince of Wales was present, as was General Allenby, who had been newly appointed to the command of the Third Army.

The next letter was written the day after the inspection although Ray seems to have lost his sense of time.

17812 Oct.26th 15
Dear Hal,
Thanks ever so much for your letter. Our Batt. starts leave today and each week the number of men will be increased, I couldn't say how they select the names. Am now out of the trenches again and am having another Army rest. I had an exceedingly hot time in the trenches last week and was not sorry to get out of them. Yes! We get our letters and parcels sent up to the trenches when we are in. Thanks very much for the tooth–ache essence, I can't get my teeth seen after out here. I am sending the notes later and am also sending by this letter a few more views and a coloured card for Ma. That's jolly good of your motor bike tyres isn't it! Thanks very much for those letters of Mabs and

Wilf they were very interesting. I haven't much more news except that we were inspected by King George and the Prince of Wales also the French President the other week. With love to all, Yrs. ever, Pud

A Field Service Postcard was written on 28th October, followed on the 29th and 30th by the following letters.

17812 Oct 29th 15
Dear Pa,
Thanks very much for your last letter. I don't think the
selection can be improved on, in my parcels, as everything that is sent is extremely useful. A pair of socks would be useful also a candle now and then also a handkerchief but am well set up for bootlaces. No! I haven't had to use the Sterilisers yet as our water has been quite good, but I always keep them handy just in case. I hope Theo will keep on his Sergt. Major job it keeps my mind a little easier as to how he is going on. I expect I shall be in the trenches again at the end of the week, we work now about 8 days in and 8 days out. We have a nice little "sausage gun" on our part of the line now and every time the Germans send one over, we send one in return. Mabs wrote and told all her exciting experiences, I should like to have been there, just to have seen a Zep. I have no more news now so will close.
With best love to all, From your loving son, Raymond.

P.S. Please tell Harold that the wrist watch is rather too much so please send another like mine.

17812 Oct.30th
Dear Hal,
Thanks very much for your letter. Have just received this weeks parcel. Have enclosed notes for last watch. The wrist watch is a bit too much so will you send one like mine. I can't stop to write any more just now. Please thank everybody for contents of parcel. With best love to all, Yrs. ever, Pud.

31–10–15 BUIRE to E3 sub–sector.
1–11–15 Trenches very bad. Nearly every available man on trench repair work or fatigues.
3–11–15 3–15p.m. Enemy fired seven light trench mortars in and around DUBLIN St., and blew in a Machine Gun dug–out killing M.G. Sergeant and one man.

Ray's next three letters, two from the trenches and one written two days after he came out on the 8th November; expand on the "matter of fact" War Diary entries.

Postmarked 4th Nov. 17812
Dear Hal,
Have received another order for a watch and leather chain for one of our Machine Gun Officers, (another watch like mine as soon as you can send it). Have sent off the notes for the other watch, you might let me know when you receive them. I haven't had much time for letters lately, as am on fatigue from morning to night in the trenches, because our Coy. is in reserve we have to fetch the rations for two Coys. about 3 miles of communication trenches. Must shut up now as I have to be up at five to start my route marches up and down the trenches again.
With love to all, Yrs. Pud.

17812 Nov. 4th.
Dear Pa,
Thanks very much for your letter. I have been having a very muddy time in the trenches, our Coy. being in reserve we have to fetch the rations for two Coys., one in the firing line and of course ourselves in the reserve. When we came in, last Sunday, it was quite fine, but the next day it commenced to rain and continued for two days. So by the third day things were very lively, and without stretching it, the mud and water came over our knees in places. Well to make things more unpleasant our beautiful dugout commenced to leak and before the day was out, we were nearly afloat, so I went hunting for another dugout, but was unsuccessful. I found a place to kip at last, in where the bombs were kept and made myself comfortable on four boxes of bombs. Will you please ask Hal to forward one of the Ingersol wrist watches, luminous dial, as I have a customer for one, (a Captain of one the of the Coys.).... Am glad you have heard from Theo and that he is all serene. Would you mind asking Chas. Kirby if he could drop me a line I should like to hear how he is getting on.
With best love to all, From your loving son, Raymond

Another contemporary account of the unpleasant fatigue work is given by Charles Douie in his book *The Weary Road*. The chapter is entitled *The City of the Dead* and gives a graphic description of an infantryman's life in the town of Albert at this time.

".... and when I had been sufficiently awakened I received orders to return at once to the La Boiselle mines on a carrying fatigue. In all the monotony of trench warfare there was no greater tedium than that of carrying parties which were needed for the supply of material to the front line trenches........The infantry soldier regarded himself as a fighting man and could not be persuaded to take kindly to the role of pack animal. Soldiers who could be relied on to remain cheerful in the most exposed trenches in the front line became unwilling and resentful on fatigue."

A further quote from this very descriptive work of Charles Douie serves as an apt introduction to Ray's next letter written on the 10th November, two days after being relieved. Having just come out of one of the Albert – La Boiselle communication trenches ".... I emerged on to it (the road) from the knee deep mud of the communication trenches.... "

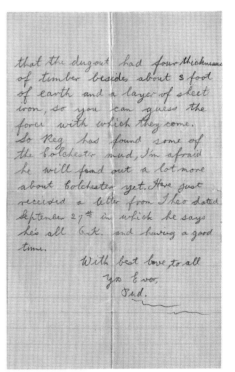

17812   Nov.10th
Dear Hal,
I have received the watch for which many thanks and am sending notes later. I have had an exceeding muddy time in the trenches last week and am now on picket duty in a town (Albert). We had about six shells over the town last night but none of them fell anywhere near me, so I didn't worry much about them. Am sorry to say we had two of our fellows killed in the trenches, by a beastly sausage which blew them to atoms. It came through the roof of a dugout and exploded as easy as coming through a piece of paper, I might say that the dugout had four thicknesses besides about 3 foot of earth and a layer of sheet iron, so you can guess the force with which they come. So Reg. has found some of the Colchester mud, I'm afraid he will find out a lot more about Colchester yet. Have just received a letter from Theo dated September 27th in which he says he's all O.K. and having a good time.
With best love to all, Yrs. ever Pud.

The Battalion was relieved by the 8th Suffolks on the 8th November and returned to the trenches on 16th November. In this period the Battalion helped build the USNA redoubt and the Albert defences. The Companies interchanged this work with physical training.

On their return to the front line the War Diary states that the trenches were "little better than when we left them".

Ray's next batch of letters from the trenches again reflect the terrible conditions, fearful bombing, shelling and sniping that occurred in what was supposedly a quiet period in the war on the Western Front. The Battalion was serving in the same sector of trenches.

17812   Nov.18th 15
Dear Pa,
Thanks ever so much for your letter. I am now having the time of my life in the trenches after a week of rain it has started to snow and kept on for two days by which time you can guess the trenches were pretty awful. Thanks very much for the idea of top boots, we are allowed to wear them, in fact you can wear practically anything while you are in the trenches. The only drawback to those

top boots is the weight, you see my pack weighs about 70lbs now, so the boots want to be very light. Thanks ever so much for those peppermints. I like them immensely and they are so handy to carry about. I'm afraid I get rather an overdose of soap, you see the only time I'm able to wash is when I come out of the trenches so of course I don't use a lot of soap. I have just read Theo's amusing letter in the "Post" and am glad to see he is keeping his pecker up, as I also am trying to do. The way my letters sometimes get delayed is because whenever we move in or out of the trenches they never take the letters on those days because there is no time to censor them.
With best love to all, from your loving son, Raymond.

17812   20–11–15
Dear Hal,
Thanks ever so much for your letter. We have been fearfully busy in the trenches and what with snow and rain, we have had an exciting time. I have just received the third watch for which many thanks, and will forward the notes as soon as we get out of the trenches. I have been bombing ever since I came into the trenches and have stood ankle deep in water, at the head of a sap, ten yards from the Germans, with a box of bombs by my side and my heart in my boots. Yesterday a German sniper got another of our chaps, we bombers were digging a sap into a mine crater which was 15 yds. across, and we had two chaps outside the trench on the bank of the crater with bombs in case the Germans attacked and one of them put his head up about 6 ins. too high and the sniper had him in a moment and at that short range smashed his head up completely. Well! Hal old chap for all the water, snow and frost, I am still as fit as a fiddle and hope you are the same. You ought to be able to see me now, you would laugh, I am covered from head to toe in thick clay mud and shall have to use a hard chisel and hammer to get it off.
With best love to all, Yours ever, Pud.

On the 24th Nov. the Battalion was relieved and marched to Buire. The next 3 letters, from Buire, include the one uncensored letter that Ray managed to get out of France. This was a brave if not foolhardy thing to do as it was a court martial offence.

17812   Nov.25th 15
Dear Pa,
Thanks very much for your last letter. This last spell in the trenches is the worst I have been through and have hardly had time to eat my food. Yes! we have long top boots in the trenches but there is not nearly enough to go round and it's those who get there first get them. Every parcel which you have sent has reached me so far, and I don't think the selection can be improved upon also the contents are always in good condition. I have once more left the trenches behind and am now looking forward to a little sleep which I think I deserve after having about 6 hrs for the last 8 days. I have no more news just now so will close.
With best love to all, From your loving son, Raymond.

17812 29–11–15
Dear Hal,

Thanks ever so much for your letter. When I woke up this morning I found that my mug of tea was frozen solid, I had placed it by my side overnight, so you can guess what the temperature is like. There is a rumour that the Germans have taken the last mine crater which they blew up last time we were in the trenches, if it is correct, we are in for a lively time when we go in next time. I am enclosing the notes for the 3rd watch and have not yet received the "oof" for the others. Yes! it is the heavy nature of the soil which keep the trenches under water so long and we have to use pumps in most places to get rid of the surplus water. Please thank Mr Wills for his contributions. I think the solidified Eau–de–Cologne is splendid and such a beautiful sniff. I expect Clementine is a bit tricky to get off isn't it? We had some more German planes over here yesterday and they again tried to blow up the railway but did not succeed, but they managed to blow some A.S.C.* to small pieces.
With best love to all, Yrs. ever, Pud.

* ASC = Army Service Corps (Ally Sloper's Cavalry)

The next letter, written a day later, is the one that avoided the censor's attention by travelling back to England with a comrade before being posted.

Albert, France.
30–11–15
Dear Hal,

I am sending this letter by a pal who is on leave and as you will see it has not been censored. Well Hal I take this opportunity of easing my mind as to the state of affairs out here at the present time. Albert, the town in which we are billeted when not in the trenches, is knocked to bits as you have seen by some of the photos I sent. I think France, the French people and the general conditions out here are about the rottenest you could find anywhere. I am just putting in a rough sketch of the part of the line we hold. As you will see by the sketch the line on the left is a good distance from the Germans and is fairly safe from sausages. But of course on the right is where all the fun is and Hell's Corner is the limit. When the Germans blew up their last mine the explosion filled in all our front line trenches in Hell's Corner, so we had to get on top of the trenches and dig them out again under the enemy's fire which was very pleasant, I don't think. The 8th Norfolks go into the trenches with us and are on our right and also help to hold a part of Hell's Corner but we hold the hottest part. The last part of the line we held was at Bray in the Somme district and we were relieved by the 1st Norfolks, but that is all old history. Well Hal I thought I would just let you know something which the censor wouldn't let me tell you in an ordinary letter .
With best love to all, Yours ever, Pud.

On the 2nd December the Battalion moved back to E3 sub–sector of trenches at La Boiselle. The conditions were again terrible with lots of rain and sporadic enemy fire. Men from the 19th Lancashire Fusiliers were attached for instruction. There are two letters from the trenches.

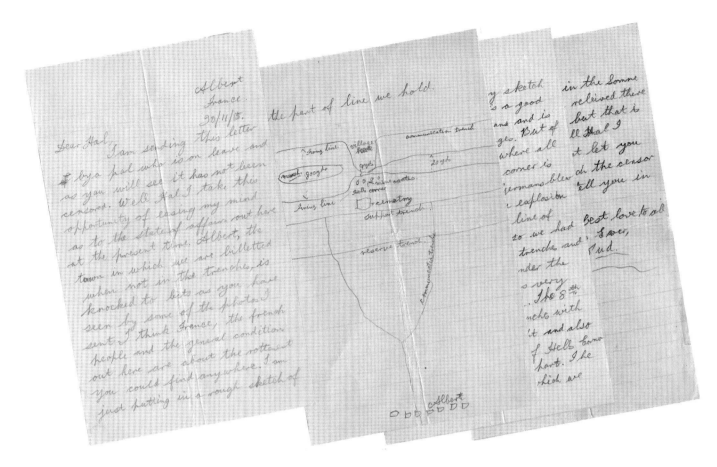

The uncensored letter referred to on the previous page.

17812 4–12–15
Dear Pa,
Thanks very much for your letter which I have just received. Re. long boots, you won't want to worry about them now as we are all issued with them and there is a pair for every man. I find the Icyclone answers very well and is a great improvement. I think the photo of Reg. is splendid and looks quite like a soldier. Well Pa I'm jolly glad we have these long boots, because this time the trenches are the worst they have ever been, and practically everywhere you walk up to your knees in mud. No! I don't think the parcels are monotonous, because you see I look forward to the same articles to replenish those already used. Our people blew a mine up yesterday and by the look of the crater I should say it gave them a nasty knock, anyway there was 4 tons of explosive in it. I am still in the best of health and have not had to visit the doctor since I have been out here. With best love to all, from your loving son, Raymond.

17812 9–12–15, From the trenches.
Dear Pa,
Have just received your letter of the 5th for which many thanks. I expect you will have received my last letter by now, I mentioned in it that every man had now a pair of top boots when in the trenches. Well Pa I think this last time in the trenches is about the worst I've experienced since my first visit to them. When we arrived in we were

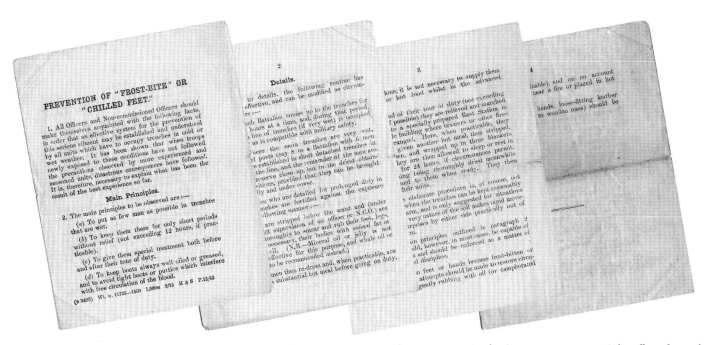

A leaflet found amongst the letters about "Prevention of Frostbite". It is illustrative of conditions being faced in the winter months.

crammed into a dug–out, which was built to hold about 30 men, (there were 50 of us), and we had to sit up and sleep. The next day the small dug–out commenced falling, as it had been raining several days and sorry to say our section Sergt. was inside of them when it fell in and was killed, this makes the second in our section. Well after 4 days in the firing line we were buzzed back to the reserve to let a part of another Batt. (which had come in for instruction) take over our part of the line. But the best is yet to be told, when we reached the reserve, we were informed that there were no dug–outs for us and we should have to sleep on the parapet, and in the rain too! Well you can guess I didn't sleep on any parapet but my pal and I set about making a dug–out which we have just completed and as we come out on Saturday, I shan't mind doing the three more nights. The Icyclone looks like lasting for ever, anyway have used it several times and it is not used much yet. No! have not yet used all the Iodine, have still plenty left. Yes! I had a good rest last time I was out of the trenches and made up for all my lost sleep. Am glad Theo is still all serene and trust he will keep so. Our guns have been giving the Germans socks now lately, we have some of the Canadian R.F.A. behind us and they make things hum.

With best love to all, from your loving son, Raymond.

Relief came on 11th December by the 19th Lancashire Fusiliers. This brought a remarkable response in Ray's correspondence home. It is all the more surprising that the comments made about this relief regiment appear to have escaped the attention of the censor .The 19th Lancashire Fusiliers are referred to in several of the following letters. A hint of the problems is given in one of the contemporary accounts.

The relief was a very difficult one on account of the state of the trenches, and matters were not improved by the fact that the unit detailed to relieve us had not been in France a fortnight.

With the 10th Essex in France

Included here are the relevant entries from the War Diaries of the 19th, 16th and 15th Lancachire Fusiliers.

19th Lancashire Fusiliers 32nd Division
Left England November 21st 1915.
3–12–15. Platoons in trenches of 10th Essex and 8th Norfolks for instruction – weather wet and mild.
11–12–15. The Battalion went into trenches and took over E3 sector from 10th Essex. Trenches in very bad condition – in many places waist deep in mud or water. Weather wet.
15–12–15. Relieved by 16th Lancashire Fusiliers.

The 16th Lancachire Fusiliers were in E3 sector from 15th to 24th December when they handed over to the 15th Lancs. Fusiliers. During that short spell the 16th Lancs. lost 15 men killed and 9 wounded (one of whom was to die on 27th December).

24–12–15. Marched to trenches section E3 La Boiselle.
24th –29th –12–15. In trenches. Battalion was very lucky to escape with only 1 man killed and 2 slightly wounded. The 19th Lancs. Fus. shared the trenches with us.
29–12–15 Relieved by 8th Suffolks.

Ray's letters with his reactions to the above are from 13th December, just after the 10th Essex was relieved.

Corbie comparisons. A postcard from before the Great War and a photo from 1985.

17812   13–12–15
Dear Hal,
Thanks very much for your letter. At last I am out of the trenches again and this time I think for a week or two, a Batt. of Fusiliers has come to relieve us. I should have said that there was a village there once as only the bare walls remain. Yes! I wear a steel helmet when bombing, all the bombers have them. We gave the Germans a shake up the last day we were in the trenches we put up a mine at 2p.m. and at the same time three batteries of artillery spoke at once and planted all the shells on the place where the mine blew up and fairly blew the Germans front line to blazes. The Regt. which relieved us are not up to much I think they are the scum of Lancashire, anyway when they came into our town, they swanked a lot and talked about getting over the parapet and taking the village in front of our trenches. But quite a different thing happened when they came up, for instance a party of them were passing one of our machine gun emplacements and it suddenly started to speak, well you should have seen them, they all dropped flat in the trench, which was about a foot deep in mud, and wouldn't get up till the gun had stopped firing. We also had to send two Sergts. and an Officer up to the trenches last night because their Sergt. couldn't get the men to keep to their posts, (these are the men who were going to get over the parapet). They are not fit to hold a

48

dummy line of trenches. No! the German planes are not much good and our planes always beat them in a scrap also they keep well out of the range of our aeroplane guns. You ought to have had some aeroplane guns like ours in London when the Zeps. came I bet they wouldn't have got away. I have enclosed a card and handkerchief for Jam (his sister Enid) as a birthday present, rather late isn't it! Must close now.
With best love to all, Yrs ever, Pud.

Corbie comparisons, 1914 and 1985. The bandstand for the Christmas Day concert no longer stands in the car park.

The 10th Essex were billeted in Albert from 12th December to 15th December, working on town defences and strengthening the Usna Redoubt. There were also bathing parties. The regimental diary indicates that they were taken right out of the area on December 15th, marching via the Ancre Valley, through Treux and Mericourt l'Abbe to La Neuville, the western suburb of Corbie. They didn't go into the trenches again until 28th December though as a later letter illustrates, Ray had expected a longer break.

17812   Dec.16th 1915.
Dear Pa,
Thanks very much for your letter which have just received. I have now moved back to about 12 miles behind the firing line and shall not be in the trenches again for about a month. You would laugh at some of the things the Regts. did which relieved us, for instance when they went up the trenches the bottoms of their coats got very muddy, well, instead of cleaning the mud off, they cut the bottoms off. Also some of them took off their packs and used them as stepping stones where–ever the water was at all deep, of course all these chaps are North country lads. The leave is still progressing but haven't heard when I am going yet, in our Coy. We are drawing for leave. We are very well supplied with clothing thanks and have a clean change about once a fortnight.
With best love to all, from your loving son, Raymond.

17812   22/12/15
Dear Hal,
Thanks very much for your interesting letter. Have received parcel quite safely and have devoured the plum pudding which was delicious. Please thank everyone for their contributions which I enjoyed very much, and thank Mr Wills for the cig. case which comes in very useful just at present as have lost my other. What do you think is the latest! Those bally Fusiliers lost two of their sentries out of a listening sap, the "huns" came and pinched them at night, lifted them bodily out of the sap, of course it must have been a planned affair on the part of the Germans but the men must also have been asleep. I saw young Jeffries just before he came home and he said he would visit you. I'm glad you didn't hurt

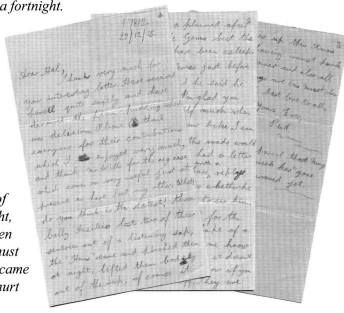

yourself much when you came off your bike, I can just imagine what the roads would be like. Have just had a letter from C. Kirby and have written a reply you might let me know whether he got it, if you happen to see him. Have enclosed the "dibs" for the other watches in the shape of a cheque, you might let me know if it is all serene, it doesn't matter about the "albert" now if you haven't sent it off. They are going to bust us up this Xmas and we are having roast pork for our Xmas dinner and also all the gift puddings are in. Must close now.
With best love to all, Yours ever, Pud.
P.S. Am afraid the parcel that May sent last Saturday week has "gone west" as it hasn't arrived yet.

From the War Diary we know that this period behind the lines was spent in Divisional training in all aspects of trench warfare, e.g. bombing, musketry, wiring, (by day and night), bayonet fighting etc. and also included mock attacks. There were also bathing excursions to Daours.

The Essex Regiment 10th Battalion

Christmas Day, the first spent abroad, was celebrated in excellent spirit. There was church parade at Corbie, after which the band occupied the bandstand in the square, and played cheerful music, subsequently heading the march to billets at La Neuville to the tune "What cheer, me old brown son, how are yer?" a popular melody with the Battalion.

Ray mentioned that Christmas dinner was due to be roast pork. This was not to be.

The Essex Regiment 10th Battalion

The chief course for dinner was to have been roast pork, but unhappily the local baker failed in his promise to bake the succulent joints and so the men had to "make do" with stew. It was a great disappointment, but Christmas pudding and the liquid accompaniment were there in unstinted measure, so that the respective feasts went quite merrily.

10th Essex War Diary

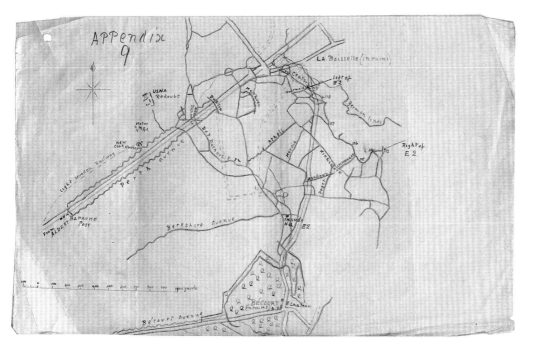

The trench map for late December 1915, part of the 10th Essex War Diary.

28–12–15. Battalion marched to Albert via Heilly.
29–12–15. Battalion marched by coys. at half hour intervals to E2 sub–sector (due north of Becourt). Owing to the two communication trenches, Becourt Avenue and Berkshire Avenue, being almost impassable, we had to march round by Meaulte, Becordel–Becourt to Becourt thence to trenches.
.... Enemy heavily bombarded our front trenches on our right in D3. A certain number of Lachrymatory shells of which we felt slight effects and wore goggles.

10th Essex War Diary

The next letter was only a short note written before the 29th December but postmarked 1st January 1916.

17812
Dear Hal,
I have just received an order for two more of the 10/6d luminous watches, can you supply them at once. I am sorry to say we are shifted back to the old line again and shall be back in the trenches again by the time you receive this letter. Haven't any more time just now.
With best love, Yrs. ever, Pud.

The next letter was written on the 7th January, the day after being relieved and billeted at Buire. It once again gives a detailed insight into Ray's view of the relieving Lancashire Fusiliers.

17812   7–1–16
Dear Hal,
Just a short letter to express my disgust at having to come back to the firing line before the appointed time. And it's all through those putrid Lancs. Fusiliers we have renamed

51

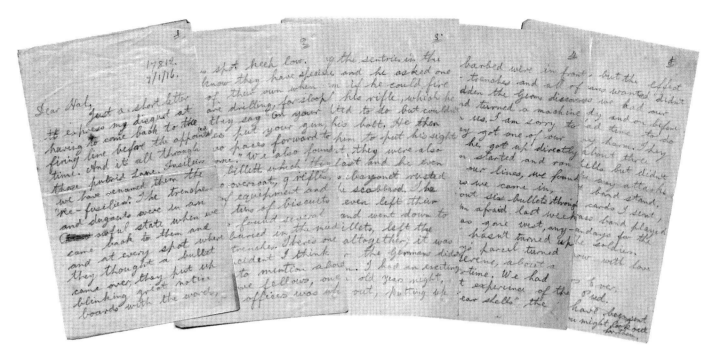

them the "Re–fusiliers". The trenches and dugouts were in an awful state when we came back to them and at every spot they thought a bullet came over, they put up blinking great notice boards with the words "Dangerous spot keep low". You know they have special orders of their own when they are drilling, for slope arms they say "On your shoulders put your gun, and two paces forward come." We also found in the billet which they left 10 overcoats, 9 rifles, 12 sets of equipment and several tins of biscuits we also found several rifles buried in the mud in the trenches. There's one little incident I think I ought to mention about these brave fellows, one of our officers was up visiting the sentries in the trenches and he asked one of them if he could fire out of his rifle, which he attempted to do but couldn't move his bolt. He then asked him to put his sight up but they were also stuck fast and he even had his bayonet rusted into the scabbard. The sentries even left their posts and went down to their billets, left the trenches altogether, it was a wonder the Germans didn't take them. I had an exciting night on old year's night ,we were out, putting up fresh barbed wire in front of our trenches and all of a sudden the Germans discovered us, and turned a machine gun on us. I am sorry to say they got one of our chaps, he got up directly the gun started and ran towards our lines, we found him as we came in, with about six bullets through him. I'm afraid last weeks parcel has gone west, anyway it hasn't turned up yet. May's parcel turned up all serene, about a week overtime. We had our first experience of the German "Tear shells" the other night, but the effect the Germans wanted didn't come off as we had our goggles ready and on before the gas had time to do our eyes any harm. They sent over about three thousand shells but didn't try to make any attack. You saw that bandstand on one of the cards I sent, well our brass band played in it on Sundays for the benefit of the soldiers. Must close now with love to all.

Yrs. ever, Pud.

P.S. The Fusiliers have been sent back to England, you might look out for them.

52

17812   8–1–16
Dear Pa,

Thanks very much for the letter. I'm afraid your last letter has gone astray. I wondered what was the matter when it didn't turn up. I have just completed another 8 days in the trenches and am once again in billets. We had to come back to the firing line because the Lancs. Fusiliers weren't capable of holding it and our officer told us today that they have been sent back to England. No! my comrades nor I have received any of the newspaper parcels. It has been dirty weather up at the trenches, which were left in a rotten condition by the last mob.... I'm glad to hear Theo is out of it for a little while, and also hope it will be a long time before he leaves Egypt. I don't know whether they will send another Div. to relieve us later on, but I hope they will so we can finish our rest. The parcel posted on the 3rd January arrived yesterday and was most welcome, please thank everyone for their contributions. I don't know whether you have sampled an army biscuit, I'm keeping one in my haversack to bring home when I come, it will come in handy as a door scraper. I think this is all just now.
With best love, from your loving son, Raymond.

One more letter was written before Ray went back to the trenches.

17812   13–1–16
Dear Hal,

Thanks very much for the letter and the watches which have just received. Have just got the parcel which was posted on Dec.27th. I thought it had gone west like Pa's letter. Yes! I am back at the same part of the line. We are expecting a big gas attack where we are, so we are getting used to putting our tube–helmets on quickly, as the gas only takes 20 secs. to travel a hundred yards. Have our troops withdrawn altogether from the Dardenelles do you know? I don't think there's a lot the matter with your bike if it took Grapes Hill, (in Norwich, Norfolk) *I think that is one of the best tests about there. We were praised up the other day by the G.C.O. who said that our Regt. was the best all round Regt. in the Div. But our Colonel is not satisfied with this, he says he is going to make it the best in the 3rd Army. All I can say is that it will be some job.*
With best love to all, Yours ever. Pud

After another period in the trenches from 15th–22nd the Battalion were relieved on the night of the 22nd January by the 6th Royal Berkshires and went by way of Berkshire Avenue into Brigade Reserve at Albert. Ray wrote one letter to his father immediately he came out of the trenches and three on successive days to Hal.

17812   Sunday Jan.23rd
Dear Pa,

Thanks very much for your letter and please excuse this letter being rather late, but I didn't have time to write in the trenches. I have received a letter from Theo written on Jan 3rd, he says my letter written to him on the 15th Nov. had only just reached him. Our section had a narrow escape the day before we came out of the trenches, we were in a small dug–out in the firing line and the Huns had started shelling when one of

them dropped about five yards off the roof of our abode and smashed a disused dug–out completely in, and also filling up the trench which leads to the dug–out, to the top. When we were clearing the trench I happened to spot the nose of the shell in the side of the bank and have it now in my pack, but I don't know how long I shall carry it as it weighs about 7lbs. and is solid brass. All the letters, parcels etc. have turned up including last weeks parcel posted on the 17th Jan. for which many thanks. I'm afraid we are not going to get released just yet so we must keep on doing our bit, and grin and bear it. The other night our guns strafed the Huns for about an hour and we got a slight idea of what a bombardment is like, the Huns replied very feebly. I don't think it will be long now before we are busy and we have one or two little surprises for the noble boshes (sic). It's surprising to relate, but it hardly rained at all the last four days in the trenches and it was beautiful moonlight. I had another gay time in front of our barbed wire and went out with our officer to see how near the German wire we could get. Well we got within 50yds. of their trenches and then were pulled up by their machine gun which started spitting, so we turned back, and I wasn't sorry when we reached our lines. I am now in a big house, I think it was an hotel in peace time, anyway it is very comfortable, in our room we have a nice fireplace with a huge mirror for an over–mantle and a table and chairs and plates, dishes, in fact we have discovered everything as the owner left it, as he had to leave in a hurry when the Huns shelled it. We have now 21 men in our platoon out of 65 which we should have and our section is 7 strong. Well Pa must close now as it is getting late and am writing this letter in bed.
With best love to all, from your loving son, Raymond.

17812   26–1–16
Dear Hal,

Thanks ever so much for your letter. Please thank Mr.Wills for the fags. The officer who I got the watches for has gone on leave so shall have to wait till he comes back for the cash, I expect it will be another cheque. We are in billets again and go into the trenches on Sunday. We have some big guns coming up the back, 15inch I think so the Huns are in for a warm time. We have just been dished out with capes, something like cycling capes, and I think they will be very useful. I say! Reg hasn't half romped through his training but expect it is because his is a draft Batt. The Huns are getting very savage along our front now, since we blew up their depot at Lille, they sent over some liquid fire a little way down on our right, when we were in last time.
With best love, Yours ever, Pud.

17812   Jan. 27th '16
Dear Hal,

Thanks for forwarding the P.C. It was from a little French kid whose acquaintance I made in _____ in the billet (sic) and I gave him my address in blighty. I think Theo has done very well in taking the Q.M. job in my opinion it is the safest job in the Regt. anyway it is in ours. Am sorry that Reg. had that spill, but am also glad to hear he hasn't hurt himself much. Please give my best respects to W.J.M. and tell him I hope to be back soon driving his old crocks. I say! it's a funny thing about that chap Thirtle, I don't know him he must be in one of the other Coy. anyway I am making enquiries and

will let you know the result. Thanks very much for the birthday parcel when it arrives. We have all got to get down cellars if the Huns start strafing us today as it Big Willie's (The Kaiser, Wilhelm's) birthday and I hope our 15 inchers will give them beans. With best love, Yrs. ever, Pud.
P.S. Longer letter next time.

17812   28–1–16
Dear Hal,
Will you please send another 10/– watch along as our S.M. wants one, as soon as poss. Yrs. ever, Pud.

Obviously Ray's little sideline of selling watches was still proving very successful – it continues throughout his time in France. He returned to the same area of trenches on 29th January 1916. His next two letters refer to incidents quoted below from contemporary accounts. The first is from the trenches and the second the day after he was relieved by the 6th Royal Berkshires. An entry in his diary gives an insight into this "active" period in the trenches.

Germans bombard our trenches on 31st '16 and come over and pinch 16 of our men, Colonel killed in the strafe.

On the night of January 31st the Battalion suffered a great loss, the commanding officer, Lieut. Colonel J.F.Radcliffe, being killed. Patrols on duty the night before reported that there was activity in the German trenches and in the afternoon the divisional 4.5 howitzers fired about fifty rounds in the direction of Mametz. The enemy retorted about 4–30p.m. upon a dump at the junction of Lochnagar Street and Kingsgate, the fire increasing in intensity until 5–15p.m. and being mainly directed upon the salient on the Battalions right front.... The hostile bombardment lifted and struck the roof of the telephonist's dug–out by a direct hit. The commanding officer and adjutant were there at the time. The roof fell in and a heavy beam struck Colonel Radcliffe, crushing his head, the other occupants, officers and signallers, escaping with a shaking.... The next day the front line dug–out was searched, when the dead Essex man was found. The casualties included, in addition to Colonel Radcliffe and a dead soldier, three others suffering from shellshock and 13 missing, subsequently ascertained to be prisoners of war.... We hated having lost men as prisoners and for a time we were disliked for our misfortunes by those in authority. This was particularly galling, after being complimented but a short time before by the G.O.C. as the best in the Division.... The loss of the Colonel was a severe misfortune. He was sitting talking to 2nd Lieut. Byerley and the Regimental Medical Officer when hit and it was afterwards recalled that at lunch that day he had been the third to light his cigarette from one match.

The Essex Regiment 10th Battalion

The Germans continued their raiding tactics a few hours later. A party of them suddenly appeared in front of the section held by the 10th Essex, clothed in British uniforms and wearing British gas masks, lulling suspicion by their use of the English language. They carried with them a red yellow and black flag, which they planted on the ramparts. It had the following inscription. "Brave British Boys. Why will you fight for your bloated capitalists, who sit at home in armchairs and send you to death?""

The Essex Regiment 10th Battalion

10th (S) Bn. Essex Regt.

Roll of Casualties for month of Jany 1916

Regtl No	Rank	and Name	Nature of Casualty	Date
17816	Pte	Harwood C	Wounded	1-1-16
13538	"	Rawlings E	Died of Wounds	—"—
17816	"	Harwood C		2-1-16
14883	"	Ward E	Shock	—"—
13385	L/Sergt	Blowers A G	Killed	3-1-16
14362	Pte	Arrowsmith G	Wounded (Self Inflicted)	4-1-16
18763	"	Tate A	Wounded	3-1-16
14476	"	Turner E	—"—	15-1-16
17783	"	Taylor H W	—"—	16-1-16
15497	"	Pay J	Wounded (Self Inflicted)	22-1-16
14534	"	Brown J	Killed	26-1-16
14899	"	Goddard G	Killed (Accidentally)	29-1-16
14564	"	Bewns G	Wounded	30-1-16
14564	"	Bewns G	Died of Wounds	—"—
10602	Lieut Col	Radcliffe J F	Killed	31-1-16
13709	Pte	Newman J	Wounded	—"—
15772	"	Ives J	Shock	—"—
3/2534	"	Fillbrooke B A	—"—	—"—
13960	"	Harris T	—"—	—"—
	"	Mark J	Wounded	—"—

Sheet No. 2

Regtl No	Rank	and Name	Casualty	Date
14286	L/Sgt	Lucas W	Missing	31-1-16
16631	L/Cpl	Archer D E	—"—	—"—
17853	L/Cpl	Foley E	—"—	—"—
14388	Pte	Wackett E	—"—	—"—
14842	Pte	Bowden J A	—"—	—"—
14534	Pte	Wood A	—"—	—"—
14186	Pte	Kimsley A	—"—	—"—
16653	Pte	French E	—"—	—"—
13762	Pte	Sharp E	—"—	—"—
14811	Pte	Gaymer H	—"—	—"—
14221	Pte	Adams J W	—"—	—"—
16579	Pte	Coote C	—"—	—"—
13635	Pte	Bewns L A	—"—	—"—

G.H.Lucas Capt & Adjt
for O.C. Major
Comdg 10th (S) Bn. Essex Regt.

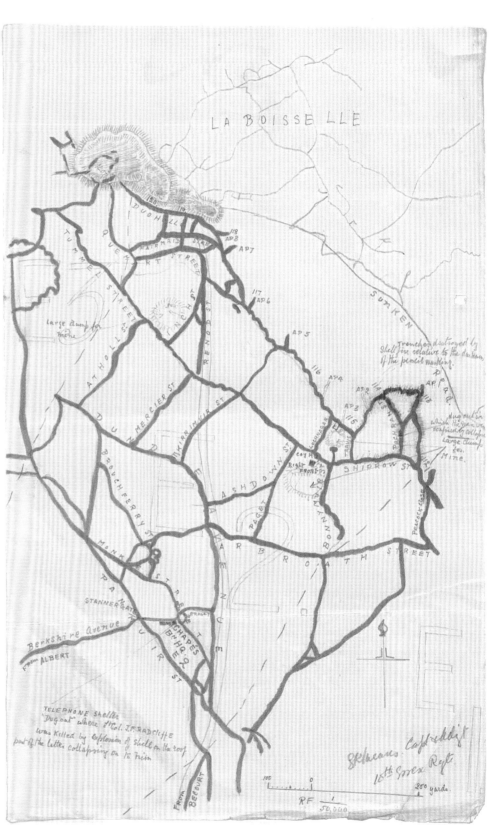

LA BOISSELLE

G.H.Lucas Capt & Adjt
10th Essex Regt.

Trenches destroyed by Shell fire relative to the darkness of the pencil marking.

Telephone Shelter "Dug out" where Lt Col J.F.RADCLIFFE was killed by explosion of shell on the roof part of the latter collapsing on to him

RF — 1/50,000

10th Essex War Diary

17812

Dear Pa,

Thanks very much for your letter and the parcels, which arrived the day before I went into the trenches. Please give my best wishes to Mr and Mrs Gee when you see them. We have had a very rough time in the trenches up to now. On the 31st Jan. the Germans gave us a terrific strafing and our Colonel was killed by a shell through his dug–out. We were in the firing line at the time which was the safest place and the only danger we were subject to was from our own shells several of which fell short and the shrapnel fell all around us but no one in our platoon was hurt. The worst part of the business was that while the bombardment was on the Huns sent a party across and pinched some of our men. Just how many we don't know yet because some of them were buried in a dug–out by a trench–mortar. They had the cheek to leave in the parapet a flag with the words on, "Our Brave British Boys." It's still a puzzle how the Germans got into our lines anyway, the 16 men are missing, they cut about 6 yds. of their own wire and of course most of ours had been knocked down by the shells. The bombardment lasted an hour and the Huns must have put over 3,000 shells, our batteries did as well as one battery alone put over 650 shells. I think it was about the hottest hour I have ever been through and it's a marvel how we came through it without a scratch. I'm glad Reg is having a little longer in England and hope I shall get my leave before he goes. Well Pa must close now as I have exhausted all the news, and I shan't be at all sorry when I get out of the trenches this time to get a little rest.

With best love to all, From your loving son, Raymond.

17812   7–2–16

Dear Hal,

Thanks very much for the letter and also the sweets you sent. Have just received the other watch. That officer hasn't returned from leave yet so I can't send the dibs yet. We have cleared up the mystery of our chaps who were pinched by the Huns during their bombardment. It appears that the Germans concentrated their fire on one part of the firing line where they intended their attacking party to come over, and knocked in the parapet at the same time burying the chaps rifles. While the chaps were digging them out with their entrenching tools, the Huns came over and of course our chaps didn't stand a chance, but we know they made a good scrap for it because the entrenching tools had blood on them and also we found about a doz. clasp knives with which they had evidently attacked the Germans. But it must have been well planned because they brought a telephone over with them and they were dressed in khaki also they passed the order down to cease fire because one of our fellows further up had started to fire on them. Those 15 inchers of ours are 4 miles behind the lines and we haven't half pasted one of the towns in front of our lines. Thanks very much for the photo of Reg. I think it is splendid. I think the last time in the trenches is the most lively one I have had so far, and two days before I came out the Germs. put up a mine gassing 20 miners and only six came out alive. My nerves are not improving very much and it's rather a difficult job to keep from being nervous if you have had many aerial torpedoes burst near you. But still I am glad to say I am A1 as regard to health and manage to keep my pecker up. I can't find out who the L/Cpl. is who visited you, his name isn't Thirtle anyway.

With best love to all, Yrs. ever, Pud.

After these letters, which herald the beginning of a much more harrowing time in this sector of the Western Front, Ray is back to the more mundane requests for watches and paying for them. The next letter is postmarked 10th February the day before Ray was promoted to Lance Corporal.

17812
Dear Hal,
Thanks ever so much for the watch and letter. I want you to send me an ordinary 5/– watch, Ingersol. I am enclosing a cheque for the two watches and 15 francs for the last watch. Am also enclosing an extra 5 francs as part payment of the 5/– watch. Will send the other 5 francs next week.
With best love, Yrs. ever, Pud.

17812   12–2–16
Dear Pa,
Thanks very much for your letter. I know now who the Lance–Corporal was who visited you, his name is Harry Ward and he is in the transport section, I knew him well before the war. He also lives at Northrepps. You will be pleased to hear that I am getting a stripe in the near future. I was rather doubtful about taking it at first because I shall be shifted out of my own platoon and it's rather hard to leave my chums who I have been with since the start. Still as I shall be in the same Coy. it won't be quite so bad. Bobbo's (Brother Wilfred's son Robert) *contributions were very pretty and please thank him for the kisses. Will you please ask Hal to let me know when he gets the cheque and note which I have forwarded for the watches. By the way! I must wish you Many Happy Returns of the day, I believe I am a bit late but I couldn't quite think of the right date. With best love, from your loving Son, Raymond.*

17812   13–2–16
Dear Hal,
Will you please forward another 10/– Ingersol with the 5/– one I ordered last. I am afraid you will have to alter the label on my parcels now as I have been presented with a stripe. Have no more news just now so will close, hoping you are in the pink.
Yrs. ever, Pud.
P.S. Have just broken the glass of my watch, can you enclose another one?

This period of relief had once again been spent in the town of Albert with the Battalion returning to the trenches on February14th. Ray sent a Field Service Postcard on 22nd February, the day he was relieved, saying he had received the letter and parcel dated 17–2–16, and would write at first opportunity. He signed the card "Pudlo No.3 Platoon".

Included here is a contemporary description of the trenches in which Ray served. Two pages from the War Diary for the period 14th–22nd February are also included. The letters that follow add to these details.

The Essex Regiment 10th Battalion

The trenches near La Boisselle were chiefly in chalk, and so held but 2 or 3 inches of mud; those farther south [where they were now] were in a heavy dark soil and so were

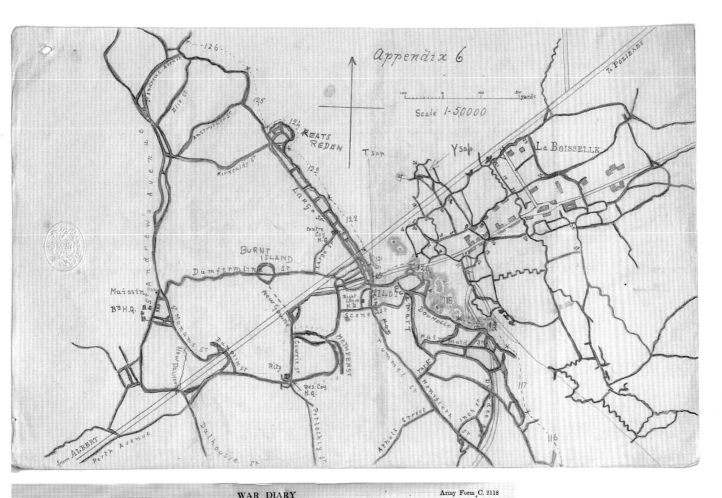

Appendix 6

Scale 1:50000

WAR DIARY
or
INTELLIGENCE SUMMARY
(Erase heading not required.)

Army Form C. 2118

Instructions regarding War Diaries and Intelligence
Summaries are contained in F. S. Regs., Part II.
and the Staff Manual respectively. Title Pages
will be prepared in manuscript.

Place	Date	Hour	Summary of Events and Information	Remarks and references to Appendices
ALBERT to Trenches E2	14/2/16		Battalion relieved 6th R¹ Berkshire Regt in Trenches, relief completed at 12.30 pm	
		4.15pm	We exploded mine in front of Fairmaid St. Blew a crater. Before the mine was exploded our 4.5" Howitzers fired for about ½ hour at German trenches in and South of La Boisselle. Immediately after explosion of mine our 18 lb opened fire with shrapnel on La Boisselle and German trenches in front of 117-120. Germans retaliated with "wizz bangs" and 6 HE on Trenches 119-121.	
		6.30pm	O.C. 185 Tunnelling Coy reported that Mine was most successful. Germans were heard working till just before the mine was exploded. Evening very quiet.	
		11.45pm	Message from Brigade warning us of possible German attack on following day.	9Kln.
Trenches	15-2-16		Morning all quiet. During afternoon our 18 lb tested new line of barrage in front of 112-116. Germans retaliated with "wizz bangs." Our Heavy Trench Mortars fired several rounds, enemy retaliated with "sausages."	
		6.10pm	Several "sausages" exploded in trenches 117-118 and knocked down about 40 yards of parapet. Our 4.5" Howitzers very slow in retaliating.	
		9.30pm	Considerable artillery action on our left about 4 miles away? Strong westerly wind during the night. Fighting Strength. officers 31 other Ranks 884	9Kln.
Trenches	16-2-16	5.15am	Strong westerly wind and rain. All quiet during the morning. During Stand to Sentry on ammunition Res. died of Tumour on Brain. During the afternoon our artillery, chiefly 18 lb, bombarded the enemys trenches in and about OVILLERS (on our left) for half an hour. All quiet during the night	9Kln.
Trenches	17-2-16	5.30	Blew westerly wind, and rain. cleared up during the morning. In the afternoon there was some reciprocal Trench Mortar activity. Enemy tried to our TM in Gowrie St out of action with wizz bangs' but did not succeed. Night all quiet.	9Kln.

1875. Wt. W593/826. 1,000,000. 4/15. J.B.C. & A. A.D.S.S./Forms/C. 2118.

10th Essex War Diary

59

Army Form C. 2118

WAR DIARY
~~or~~
~~INTELLIGENCE SUMMARY~~
(Erase heading not required.)

Instructions regarding War Diaries and Intelligence Summaries are contained in F. S. Regs., Part II. and the Staff Manual respectively. Title Pages will be prepared in manuscript.

Place	Date	Hour	Summary of Events and Information	Remarks and references to Appendices
Trenches E 2	18-2-16	2 am	Lively cannonade about 2 or 3 miles to our left.	
		3 am	Enemy fired 11 "sausages" several into left of E2. Our 4·5" Howitzers replied with 9 rounds. No more "sausage."	
			All quiet during the morning, except for Rifle grenades on our left front. 3 men wounded.	
			During the afternoon reciprocal trench mortar activity. Our 2" mortar gun replied effectively	
			Night quiet.	
Trenches E 2	19-2-16		Strong N.W. wind.	
			Rifle grenades exchanged freely.	
		11 am	The enemy first shelled Gowrie St with about 40 shells and then commenced a 20 minute intense mortar bombardment several salvos of large "Sausages". Our 4·5" Howitzer retaliated. Rest of day quiet except for Rifle Grenades on left	
		6 pm 6·45 pm	Heavy bombardment about 5 miles to the North.	
		10·15 pm	A salvo of "Sausages" on our left front, could not get any retaliation by our 4·5" Howitzer.	
			A great many lights sent up by the enemy during the night behind La Boisselle. Red, green, & white lights. There seemed to have some connection in aircraft for a Zeppelin (?) went over Eastwards at 11·50 pm, it was heard for 20 minutes but not seen.	
		12 mn	German working party heard and seen in German lines in front of trench 116. Our 18 lbs fired 3 rounds gun fire on to the point.	
			Remainder of night quiet.	
Trenches E 2	20-2-16		Slight NNE wind. Slight artillery activity during day. 2 M.G. (Maxim) brought up by M.G. Coy in the evening one to DUNDEE Av. and one to ARBROATH St. Night quiet except for a few Rifle grenades.	

1873 Wt W593/826 1,000,000 4/15 J.B.C. & A. A.D.S.S./Forms/C. 2118.

---

deep in mud. Only the tallest men were able to pass along this front line in high waders and get no liquid mud in their boots. The Colonel was a little man and he disappeared in the mud to a point quite half–way up his stomach. The front line was the worst. Company headquarters at one point were under a huge mine shaft dump about 100 yds from the front line, a colossal mountain of white chalk burrowed from the bowels of the earth. This was the well known Lochnager Sap, which was successfully excavated at three different levels right under the enemy's front and support lines, and which shook him up more than a little when it was put up on July 1st, 1916.

No.3 Platoon   17812   24–2–16

Dear Pa,

Thanks very much for your welcome letter. I'm glad to hear Theo is coming home, I think he has done his bit and can do with a little holiday. I had a rotten time in the trenches last time as most of them were feet deep in mud and water and quite a number of our chaps got trench feet. I had an interesting night out looking for a German sniper, there were six of us and an officer and we crawled about two hundred yards along the German barbed wire and picked up a complete set of German equipment which laid about five yards from their wire. But we couldn't find the sniper, so we gave it up and went back to our trenches. I can't remember that chap Nockels' christian name, but he was a fisherman and a little, short chap. .... The flash lamp and lighter are progressing alright but the watch glass is a trifle large. The 5/– Ingersol Hal. sent off hasn't turned up yet.

With best love to all, from your loving son, Raymond.

(Postmarked 25th Feb.)

No.3 Platoon   17812

Dear Hal,

Thanks very much for the letter and also the 10/– Ingersol which arrived while I was in the trenches. I'm sorry to say the glass nor bezel will fit my watch as they are a trifle large. By the way did you get the cheque and 4 five franc notes I sent? Have not yet received the 5/– Ingersol I'm afraid it has gone astray. I have been shifted into No.3 Platoon and am getting used to it gradually. Had a rotten spell in the trenches last time, most of the time wading about knee deep in water. Hoping you are in the pink. Yrs. ever, Pud.

On February 29th the 18th Division was moved out of the line and the 53rd Brigade marched along the Albert–Amiens road, under the keen eye of General Maxse, into billets at Franvillers. The 10th Battalion Essex Regiment did not return to the same section of trenches but were destined to move to a section further south, close to the valley of the river Somme.

Ray's next 4 letters were from the billets at Franvillers and reflect a more relaxed atmosphere.

No.3 Platoon   17812   Mar.3rd '16
Dear Pa,
Thanks very much for your letter, I expect you will have received my other one by now. You will be pleased to hear that we have once more shifted back from the firing line for another rest and I hope it won't be broken into this time. I'm sorry I didn't write sooner last time, but it wasn't possible when we were in the trenches last, because of the work and condition of the weather. The snow has now nearly all disappeared and we have once more settled down to the French rainy weather. I mentioned in the last letter that the bezel and glass were a trifle large and the glass wouldn't fit the old bezel. I haven't quite finished the Icyclone but shan't require any more just yet as I am out of the trenches for a while. The tinder lighter is still in working order also the watch, but am sorry to say I have jiggered up my flash lamp altogether, but I think he has done good service and I can't grumble at it refusing to work. It's rather rough on Ralph Salter after being out since May, but hope he soon may get his leave, as I hope to get mine one day. With best love to all, from your loving son, Raymond.

17812   9–3–16
Dear Pa,
Thanks very much for your letter. Yes! I heard a week ago that all leave had been stopped but am hoping that it won't be for long. I am very sorry to hear that Ma is laid up but hope she will soon recover. Yes! I am well furnished against the cold and wet and now get plenty of clean clothing. I heard some time ago about the Old Tower at the Garden of Sleep going, it was in one of the Norfolk papers. Young Abbs is in the same village as the one I am billeted in , at an R.A.M.C.* dressing station, I haven't seen him yet, but one of the Northrepps chaps has, and I hear he is now a Corporal. There's not much news to tell you this time, we have been drilling, eating and sleeping most of the time we have been here.
With best love to all, from your loving son, Raymond.

* Royal Army Medical Corps

17812   9–3–16
Dear Hal,
Thanks very much for your letter. The long lost Ingersol has not yet arrived so am afraid it has gone west. I have enclosed 3 five franc notes for the last 10/– watch. I think the contents of the parcels cannot be bettered, so if you don't mind just carrying on as usual, is all I ask, thanking the contributors most heartily. We have been drilling and firing on an improvised range down here for the past week and am glad to say we have not been overworked. Please give my best wishes to Mr Hardy and his Misses.(sic). The weather is still frosty and snowyfied (sic) but still I can't grumble now I am out of the trenches. Was very sorry to hear Mrs Wills was ill and hope she will soon be better. Nothing much doing now, except that I saw the R.A.M.C. erecting about a doz. large tents for casualty clearing stations. Hoping you are in the pink.
With best love, Yrs. ever, Pud.

While not being dated, the following letter was written before the 14th March 1916, the date the Battalion moved forward once again.

17812   ?/3/16   Dear Hal,
Thanks very much for your last letter and the watches which arrived safely. I am shifting back to the trenches again soon and to a new part of the line. That 5/– Ingersol is the only parcel I have lost since I have been out here, so the rotten thing has broken my record. I expect you will have received the other 3 five franc notes by now, if they haven't gone astray. I managed to fit up with the watch glasses thanks, but if you could send me a case to fit the Ingersol I think it would save a lot of broken glasses. Well Hal the weather has now broken up and the sun once more smiles upon us, in fact it has been quite hot the last day or two. I am sorry for Reg, as I saw something of the Plassey, during my prolonged stay in Colchester. I have been spending most of my time, and incidentally money, in an estaminet, drinking coffee, as there isn't much else to do and with a nice tart to sit and admire, I find it very elevating. I hear leave is starting again soon and perhaps I shall stand a chance later on, anyway "while there's life there's soap." Am glad you didn't hurt yourself when you had that skid, I expect the roads have been in an awful state. Am jolly glad to hear Mrs W. is much better and hope she will speedily recover. I am enclosing another photo for you as I thought perhaps you would like one. Must close now.
With best love to all, Yrs. ever, Pud.

The Battalion marched to Etinehem Camp on March 14th and two days later they took over a section of line at Maricourt from the 20th (King's) Liverpool Regiment. The Battalion had the 8th Suffolk and 11th Royal Fusiliers on the right and left respectively, with the 8th Norfolk in support.

The Essex Regiment 10th Battalion

The 10th Essex held the Northern and Eastern edges of Maricourt Wood, from the north–eastern corner of which a sap ran within thirty yards of the enemy trench. The garrison, three sections of a platoon, were not unduly worried, their chief anxiety being as to whether the enemy shelling would block the communication trench. At the other end of the line was Machine Gun Wood, the comparative quiet of which is best

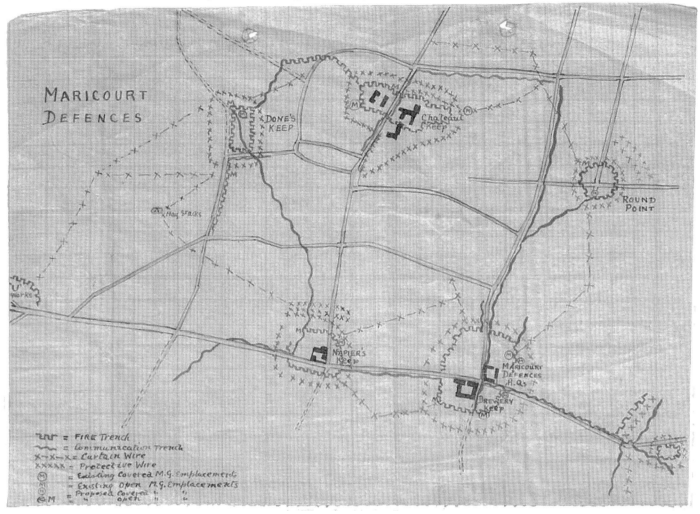

MARICOURT
DEFENCES

DONE'S KEEP
Chateau Keep
ROUND POINT
Hay Stacks
U WORKS
NAPIER'S KEEP
MARICOURT DEFENCES H.Qs
BREWERY KEEP

᠁ = FIRE Trench
⌇ = Communication Trench
X—X—X = Curtain Wire
XXXXX = Protective Wire
Ⓜ = Existing Covered M.G. Emplacements
Ⓜ = Existing Open M.G. Emplacements
ⓂM = Proposed Covered "   "
    "   open   "   "

recalled by the names which were bestowed—"Honeymoon Lane" and "Cushy Corner."
Colchester, too, was not forgotten, for some of the earthen ways were called "Long
Wyre Street", "Lexden Road" and "Abbey Fields". In the woods the foliage was so thick
it was possible to walk about in security during daylight hours and pluck primroses,
bluebells and willow catkins. The Battalion went into support at Maricourt on March 21st
and the Norfolks marched to Etinehem. The village (Maricourt) had been extensively
damaged by shellfire, but billets were fairly comfortable, particularly at the chateau,
which was so soundly constructed that the ground floor was still in use. The men were
chiefly employed in improving the communication trenches and rat–hunting, the latter a
diversion for the whole Division.

There are several letters from Ray before the Battalion marched to Etinehem via
Bronfay Farm and Bray on April 2nd.

17812   17–3–16
Dear Pa,
Thanks very much for your letter. I am once more back to the firing line and on a new

*The detailed trench
map of the Maricourt
defences, March 1915.*

*Bronfay Farm 2007. The
owner explained that
war reparations paid
for the second storey
on the farmhouse.*

Maricourt 2007. This home was once the Battalion headquarters.

The War Diary map of the Maricourt Defences dated August 1916.

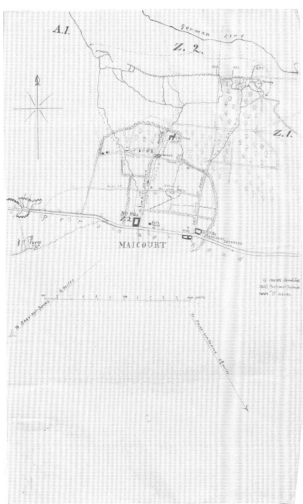

part of the line, but am glad to say it is not so warm as the last part we left. But of course it will not remain quiet for long now we are here as the Essex are noted for stirring things up. We are at present in reserve in a village which has suffered from Fritz shells and every little while they send a few shrapnel shells over just to let us know they are still there. There's one good point so far about this part of the line there are no "mines" or "sausages". Hal said he was enclosing another 5/– Ingersol in the parcel but presume he forgot to enclose it, as it hasn't arrived. I hope Hal managed to get exempted, I think they ought to allow one of the family to keep out of it. ....
Must excuse short letter but haven't much time for writing now.
With best love to all, from your loving son. Raymond

.

Ray's brother Harold, Hal, was the one of the five brothers that their father succeeded in keeping from serving at the front for most of the war by applying for exemption for service. He argued that he would have been unable to run the family electrical business without at least one of his sons to assist. Harold did finally join up at the end of the war and served in the newly–formed Royal Air Force.

17812   17–3–16
Dear Hal,
Will you please send another 10/– watch as well as the 18/6 one I ordered. We are having lovely weather now and have also moved up near the firing line. I can't stop to write much now so will excuse this short note.
Yrs. ever, Pud.

17812   22–3–16
Dear Hal,
Thanks ever so much for your letter and watch which arrived yesterday. I am glad to say the weather has bucked up a bit and the sun has actually smiled on us. I have once more returned to the trenches and Fritz but on a quieter part of the line, and am glad to say, so far we have not experienced any "mines" or "sausages" on this part. But you can bet your life we shan't be here long before we start strafing the Huns and then the fun will begin. Oh! by the way we had a shell through the roof of our house, only as luck would have it, I happened to be in the cellar where I repair when they start chucking old iron about. We use the village, where I am at present, as a reserve for the firing line and as it is only 300 yds. from the Huns, you can guess it is pretty warm, anyway some of the houses look as if they were drunk. I was jolly glad to see by the "Post" that you obtained your exemption as it would have made a rotten mess up if you hadn't. Still I can quite realise how keen you must be to get into khaki and your part in the game is a lot harder than mine to bear, but cheer up and let's hope the rotten war will soon be over. It was the same

division that relieved us last time but the Lancs. Fusiliers were missing. Please thank May for the fags, it was a pleasure to smoke a decent fag again and wish Mrs Wills many happy returns from me. Please tell little Billy I will write later as haven't had a lot of time lately and hope she is getting better. Have just had an amusing letter from Theo which was written on the 8th March and he appears to be all o.k. Do you know what part of the globe Reg has gone to? Just at present this line is what I call a picnic and six inch shrapnel shells are the only things we have to put up with but of course things may alter later on when the "Shiny Tenth" get into working order. I have just been talking to young "Lifter" Bly of 8th Norfolks have also seen "Loady" Nockels and you might tell Mr Gee that I have seen his son–in –law if you happen to see him. Well Hal must close now hoping you are in the pink and that you liked the photo I sent of our platoon.
With much love, Yrs ever, Pud

The boys of No. 3 Platoon, 10th Essex Regiment, France. Ray in on the right of the back row, without a sheepskin.

17812   23–3–16
Dear Pa,
Thanks ever so much for your letter. I'm glad you liked the photo, it was taken just after we came out of the trenches. Am still in the trenches, we do a little longer in the trenches now, because this part of the line is quieter, just at present. I tumbled to the chaps who were in front of the tribunal although no names were mentioned, and am jolly glad to hear Hal was exempted.... The weather here is still keeping fairly fine and it isn't a bit cold now. Thanks very much for Fred Love's address, I had a letter from him a little while ago and he seems to be having a good time, but the silly chump wants to come out here. Tonight while I am writing this letter, the Huns are very quiet and only now and then can a shot be heard. Well Pa must conclude now.
With best love, from your loving son, Raymond.

P.S. I suppose you don't know what Regt. young Davison is in? I haven't come across him yet. I saw young Jefferies and Russel Hunt also George Rook yesterday and appeared to be doing well.

On the evening of the 2nd April the Battalion marched to Etinehem via Bronfay Farm and Bray, with platoons at 200 yard intervals. It was a long and tedious task and the last platoon did not arrive at its destination until 3a.m. The 10th Essex were in divisional reserve and during the short stay particular attention was paid to gas warfare. On April 8th another move was made to the trenches this time by way of Bray, Suzanne and Maricourt Valley.

10th Essex War Diary

11–4–16 2p.m. Enemy fire 19 shells, 4.2in. Howitzers, into A.P.1, some damage done to the trench, 2 men killed and 2 wounded by this fire.

This war diary entry is included because the postscript in Ray's next letter refers to this incident. The letter is undated but was certainly written around this time. It is followed by another short undated note also written about this time.

17812   Dear Hal,
Thanks very much for your letter. I have received all the watches you sent and will send the cash as soon as I receive it. Thanks very much for the overcase for my watch which I received all serene. I am now doing 6 days in the firing line after doing 12 days in reserve. Of course we have had several casualties, the Essex always does, and they have mostly been from shrapnel. Our division has now been allotted a special job, namely relieving division, we travel up and down the line relieving different Regts. to allow them to go back for a rest and we shall get ours in spasms. I saw an interesting scrap between a German Fokker and a French battle plane the other day, it ended by the Frenchman getting above the Fokker and pouring his machine–gun fire down on to him, the Fokker then turned elegantly upside down and descended to earth slightly bent. I have enclosed a cheque for one pound and 50 francs you might let me know whether I am still in debt. We have had some more snow and frost but today it is quite like summer and I hope it will continue to keep so. Well Hal have no more news just now so will shut up. Hoping you are keeping in the pink, and by the way as regards the wrist strap, I found that I was in danger of breaking the watch when at work so I left it off.
With best love, Yrs. ever, Pud.
P.S. Have just heard that five of the chaps in my old platoon (No.1) have been hit by shrapnel and that most of them are "blighty" cases. (No such luck ever comes my way). Have just received your last letter please thank Mr Wills for the sweets and cigar. The writing pad is plenty you sent, only I haven't always got it by me.

17812
Dear Hal,
Please send two more Ingersol 10/– watches if you have them. I am still in the pink and will write later.
With best love, Yrs. ever, Pud.

The Battalion were relieved on the 15th April and took over the Maricourt defences once again.

17812 16–4–16   Dear Pa,
Thanks ever so much for your letter which have just received. I am sorry to say leave is stopped again and I think it will be some time because we are expecting something to come off. I should very much like my leave while Theo is at home but am afraid it will not be possible. We have been expecting a gas attack now lately but am glad to say it hasn't come off yet, and I hope I'm not in the trenches when it does happen. I have been acting full rank in the trenches this time and have been doing duty with the senior N.C.O.'s which I may say is much pleasanter than doing sentry duty on the fire step. Yes! My periscope is still in first class order but haven't used it in these new lines yet as there is no need because you can look over quite safely. Have been progressing very well up to the present as an N.C.O. but of course I have a lot to learn yet. Shall have to close now.
With best love from your loving son, Raymond.

17812 16–4–16
Dear Hal,
Thanks very much for your letter. Am glad you received the splosh all right. I think Theo and Reg were both very lucky to meet each other and am very glad they were able to. Those blighters at the War Office have stopped our leave again, I expect they have got the "wind up". I am acting full Corp. in the trenches this time and don't do any sentry duty on the fire step, my job is to visit the sentries and to shove up star–lights every now and then, just to make sure the Huns are not making a raid. I was wakened on Thursday morning about 1-30a.m. by the banging of shells and crashing of "sausages", the Germs. were bombarding the Regt. on our left and they made three raids during the bombardment, two were repulsed but the third got into their trenches and captured some of their men but they managed to collar one Hun. The bombardment lasted about an hour and a half and the Huns buzzed over about four thousand shells besides several other varieties of explosives. We have just completed six days in the firing line and are now changing into a redoubt for another six days. We were out on patrol (myself and another chap) in front of our wire the other night and we found a German helmet but there happened to be a German head in it and as we couldn't extract it, we had to leave our beautiful souvenir out there which was a beastly shame. I expect you will have got my order for two more 10/– watches but in case you haven't I thought I should mention it. I can't think of anything else to write about just now. Please thank Taffy for the chocs. With best love to all, Yrs. ever, Pud.

On 21st April 1916 it was back to the trenches in Z.2 sub–sector (see map page 64) to be relieved by 2nd Bedfordshire Regiment on the 29th April. The Battalion marched to Etinehem into divisional reserve.

There are two letters from the trenches at this time.

17812   22–4–16
Dear Pa,

*Thanks very much for your letter. The Icyclone arrived all serene but I didn't discover
the Iodine, I expect it got mislaid, I am still in the redoubt but am moving out tomorrow
into the counter–attack Coys. place for another six days. Oh! by the way could you send
me a bottle of Bisurated Magnesia tablets as I suffer from heartburn a lot and some
of my chums have used the above remedy for it and found it successful. The weather
has been very showery now lately but the sun doesn't forget to shine now and again. I
am sorry to say one of my chums was killed by a shell yesterday, it makes you realise
the rottenness of war when someone is bowled over who you have been pals with. The
Huns again bombarded on our left this making the third one since we have been in
the trenches this time. I have exhausted my Harrisons Nursery Pomade, so I could do
with another tin if you could send one. Am glad to hear Ma and Syb. are progressing
favourably and hope they will soon recover. We are expecting to get relieved from this
front shortly and I suppose we shall go to a fresh part of the line and relieve another
division. Must close now.*
With best love to all, From your loving son, Raymond.

17812   27–4–16
Dear Hal,

*Have received both watches safely and am enclosing cheque for same, if you should
have any difficulty changing it the Officer is going to pay me in cash so you might let
me know, if you have any. I had an exciting time the other afternoon, we were digging
in a support trench and throwing the earth over the parapet and didn't notice at the
time that the Germans had a "spotter" or observation balloon up and of course it soon
spotted us. Well in the three minutes the shelling lasted, I should think they sent about
50, and these being all sizes from 4.7s to whizz–bangs. But the most exciting part was,
of course when we made a bee–line for the nearest dug–out, and to get to it we had to
pass through the hottest part of the shelling. Well just as we all rushed down the trench
a four point seven crashed through the parapet and fell right across the bottom of the
trench and as luck would have it, didn't explode, or I shouldn't be writing this, and we
all had to hop over it expecting every minute to be blown to atoms, I can tell you it's
the warmest three minutes I have ever been through. I should think they had about six
batteries trained on about 50 yards of trenches. Well Hal by the time you receive this
letter I shall be out of these trenches and on our way back for another short rest after
which we shall seek fresh hunting grounds in another part of the line. I may as well tell
you that it is a great honour to be a flying Division and it is only given to divisions of
which they are certain that they can hold any part of the line, hot or otherwise. I am
sorry to hear Clementine is again on the sick list that Mag. seems to have been a lot
of trouble. The same Division is coming back which we relieved for their rest, but am
afraid they will notice a change in their line and am also afraid they will say things
about us. It was possible when we relieved them to walk over the top in parts into the
firing line, but now you mustn't even show your little finger. The weather has again
brightened up and once more the sun shines and the lark larks. I expect you have read
about the Russians being brought over here, I fancy we shall make the dirty Huns sit up*

before the winter is again with us. Well Hal must close this short letter and have another go at digging.
With best love to all, Yrs. ever, Pud.
P.S. Could you send me a small pocket book for taking notes s'il vous plait.

The next letter was written on the 29th April, the day the Battalion was relieved. Ray obviously didn't know that relief was imminent.

17812 29–4–16
Dear Pa,
Thanks very much for your welcome letter. We are doing a little extra in the trenches waiting for the other division, we have now done three weeks in and in that period I have had two washes and one shave, which is quite good for the firing line. Have received both watches and Iodine and have sent a cheque off for the same. Yes! I am well provided against gas, we have two of the latest tube–helmets, which have been tested through gas ten times stronger than that which the Germans use. I have enclosed a small paper of directions, which are enclosed in the tube–helmet. We have also goggles for use against Lachrymatory (tear) shells and they have also been proved successful. The only difficulty in a gas attack is getting the helmets on quick enough, as with a light breeze the gas travels at a rate of a hundred yards in 20 seconds, still we have had plenty of practice and hope to pull through alright if ever they should make an attack. On Thursday morning at about 1 a.m. our guns made a big strafe on the Germans and two raiding parties were sent out by our division one being successful and capturing several prisoners, but the other one came back without any. It was terrific while it lasted and I began to feel sorry for the Huns if they happened to be in the trenches "standing to". I am glad to hear Sybil is out of hospital and hope she will soon be all serene. The Rev. Hamilton, when he sent me an Easter card, mentioned about Norman Bastow being killed of which I was very sorry to hear. But after being out here a little while one looks on death as a matter of course and everyone seems to get quite callous. I was very pleased to hear Ma is a little better and hope the warm weather will continue so as to complete her cure. Thanks very much for the St. John Ambulance report, it was very interesting and is a real credit to Cromer and to the members in it. I say! that was smart work getting Miss Spinks from Runton to the hospital, still of course Hal was in the team which makes all the difference. As to a bath, they are few and far between now we have shifted from our old line but hope to be better provided when we get out.
With best love to all, from your loving son, Raymond.

On 30th April Ray's company was in Bray assisting in the construction of a light railway two miles north–east of the town. On the 4th May all ranks marched to Sailly, where the night was spent, and arrived at Longpré, one and a half miles north–west of Amiens, on May 5th.

The next letters were written just three days before Ray went home for 10 days leave. He wasn't expecting it to come so soon! He probably got home before the letters!

Ray's father was a founder member of the St. John Ambulance Division at home in Cromer and all his sons had been members. At that time, and until the 1960s, St John or Red Cross Divisions operated all local ambulance services.

The light railway continues to run from Froissey, near Bray.

17812   7–5–16
Dear Pa,

*Thanks ever so much for your letter. I have now shifted well back from the firing line,
but the march knocked me up a good deal as 20 miles with a 70lb pack naturally would
do after being 3 weeks in the trenches. I am very glad to hear Theo is home and that he
looks well, I expect he is very brown! It's quite a change to be away from the war zone
and to see electric light. I am glad to hear Ma is better and hope she takes her trip into
the country. I am just about to be inoculated again and this time we have the two doses
in one and by the look of some of the chaps who have already been done, I should say I
am in for a rough time. I expect to be home in about a month's time if nothing occurs to
stop me. Well Pa news is scarce just now so must close with best love.*
From your loving son, Raymond.

17812   May 7th 1916
Dear Hal,

*Thanks very much for your letter. I received the Pomade and Magnesia for which many
thanks. Have now shifted back to 20 miles behind the firing line and am billeted in a big
city, it's quite a treat to see trams and electric light again. Hope you received the cheque
all serene! Have just picked for leave and expect to be home in three weeks or a month,
if it's not stopped. Yes! the tin of fruit was a welcome and should like one now and
then. Of course I can't say exactly when I shall be home but have picked fourth on the
N.C.O.'s list and as they go every five days, I don't think I shall be long, but of course
they will persist in stopping the leave every now and then. Well Hal no more exciting
news this time so will dry up. Hoping you are in the pink.*
With best love to all, Yrs. ever, Pud.

*On leave. Ray,
now with his lance
corporal's stripe, is
on the right. In the
centre is brother
Theo, returned from
Gallipoli. On the left is
eldest brother Wilfred,
who served on anti-
Zeppelin and aircraft
defences.*

Ray came home on leave on May 10th. His sister Enid remembered him coming home and that "mother had enormous trouble because he was flea ridden". There was clearly time for some photographs during his leave.

On the left, Ray is with his sister in law Nell and brother Theo; on the right he is with his mother Clara.

The precious leave pass and rail ticket.

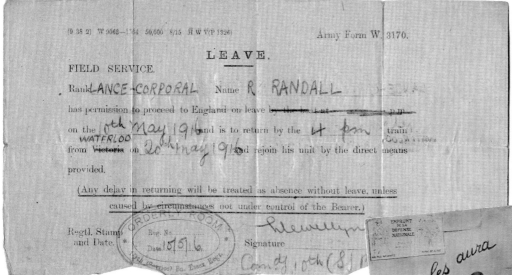

Ray's first communication after returning to France on 20th May was a postcard postmarked 27th May but written before the 23rd.

Dear Hal,
Have arrived safely back in sunny France and will write later as have not much time now.
Yrs. ever, Pud

On 23rd May the Battalion marched from Longpre to Corbie by way of Daours. Headquarters and 2 Coys, the next day went to Bronfay Farm in relief of 6th Royal Berks. and 2 Coys. constituting brigade reserve were moved from Corbie to Bray, and then on 25th to Billon Wood to succeed the 2 Coys. of the Berks. there. Bronfay Farm consisted of a considerable range of buildings in an isolated spot on the Bronfay Farm – Bray – Maricourt road and which although a mile and a half from the line, had suffered little from hostile bombardment. It proved a comfortable H.Q. and was a noted centre of hospitality. "A" Company was attached to the 280th Field Company R.E. for work on the Straw line, "B" Company was employed on mining fatigue at Carnoy and "C" & "D" Companies assisted 79th Field Company R.E. to construct Spring Ave., a communication trench over a mile Long ,which ran from the centre of Billon Wood to Carnoy.

On the 26th May Ray sent a short note with a request to obviously settle an argument. Matters concerning football were still important.

17812   26–5–16
Dear Hal,
Can you send me a football guide, I want to find out who were playing in the County teams in 1909–1910–1911. Hoping you are all serene.
Yrs. ever, Pud.

The next two communications reflect the depression that many soldiers must have gone through after having spent a period of time at home on leave. It was a different world to have been at home in Cromer with family and friends where there would be little real indication that an horrific war was going on. Within twenty four hours of having the comforts and security of home life Ray was again experiencing the discomfort and privations of front line trench warfare. The Field Postcard dated 28–5–16 gives the impression that Ray expected or hoped to be discharged soon.

On June 2nd the 10th Essex relieved the 8th Battalion Suffolk Regiment in Sub. Sector A1 (Carnoy) and Ray's company went into the front line.

The letter following, dated the following day, gives a vivid description of a mine explosion. In this case it is an enemy mine that has been placed by tunneling under the British lines.

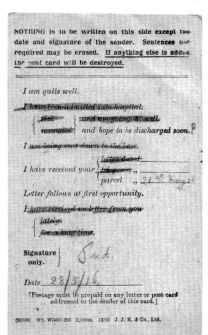

17812   3–6–16
Dear Hal,
Thanks very much for your letter and parcel which has just arrived. I am once again back to the line, but am in the "sausage" and mine area again. Didn't you get my postcard ? Yes! I am settling down fairly well now, and hardly realise that I have been to "blighty". The weather has been lovely now lately, so of course the trenches are in decent condition. Please thank everyone concerned in the parcel, I didn't half make the boys jealous with the cigar, which arrived in the first one. I feel in the mind for writing just now so will just describe what happened the first

night we got back to the trenches. By the way you often see in the papers "a little mining activity" on such and such a front, this is what really happens. The first night we were in the trenches the Huns put up a mine, and owing to the closeness of the trenches they damaged their own as well as ours. I happened to be about 50 yds. to the right of the scene of the explosion and so got a decent view. The first I felt of it was a sudden tremor, it was just like being in a small boat in a squall. After several seconds which seem hours, the ground suddenly yawned open, a huge sheet of flame shoots up in the air, hot gasses, yellow and white rush out. At the same instant almost, our machine–guns and riflemen sweep the crater which has just been formed, and our artillery pour shrapnel and high explosives into their supports, while the Germans do likewise to ours. Then over the top come a few Huns, making for the crater several of them got potted and the rest either evaporated or returned. This unholy row is maintained for about an hour or so, and everyone is highly strung, and all night long both sides are watching to prevent the other from occupying the lips of the crater. After a night on the qui vive with no sleep, the following day is given over to trench mortaring. Recollect the phrase, "a little mining activity"! Well Hal I expect you will find this very dry reading, but it was all I could think of to write about. Hoping you are in the pink.
With love to all, Yrs. ever, Pud.
P.S. Please distribute cards enclosed.

On June 10th the Battalion went back to Bray upon relief by the 8th Surrey of the 55th Brigade. For ten days the companies were distributed as working parties. They dug a deep cable trench between Billon Wood and Maricourt, worked under O.C. Divisional Signals in laying a cable line, dug in Billon Wood under 79th Company, R.E., and unloaded barges at Bray. All ranks were keyed up for the offensive now close at hand.

June 8th to June 25th was for the men a period of extremely hard and tiring manual labour.

17812   11–6–16
Dear Pa,
Thanks ever so much for letters and parcels which have just arrived. Have just come out of the trenches again for a short rest after an exciting time in. Could do with another bottle of Magnesia tablets, as have just finished the others. Will you please ask Hal to get me the 1912 football annual if he can and thank him very much for the others. The weather is inclined to be rather damp again and the two days in the trenches were not very pleasant on account of the mud. I hope you enjoyed yourself in town as I am sure you did, and trust you are now feeling better for your short holiday. Well Pa must conclude now.
With best love to all, from your loving son, Raymond.

17812
Dear Pa,
Thanks muchly for your letter. We have been on fatigue ever since we have been out of the trenches and have had some very exciting times. We are not allowed to give much news now, and they have also stopped "green" envelopes, as some of the chaps have

The town of Bray

Froissey, near Bray, where a short canal cuts across a loop of the river Somme. Barges brought supplies for transfer to the light railway to the front.

been foolish enough to put in information useful to the enemy. The French have just altered their clocks so their time is now the same as our own. My comrades were all serene when I returned off leave, and of course they were eager for news from "blighty". I shall now be able to get a job as a steam winch driver, as I worked on the barge we unloaded the other day, while on fatigue. One more trade the Army has taught me. Am glad to hear you are all serene at home and am glad to say I am the same. I haven't heard from Reg since he has been out and I don't know his address. Must conclude now.
With best love to all, from your loving son, Raymond.

17812   17–6–16
Dear Hal,
Thanks ever so much for your letter and parcel which has just arrived. You mustn't be surprised if you don't hear from me in a little while, but the papers will most likely supply the information. Yes! Have received the snaps from May and think they are very decent. The annuals you sent had not the name in I was looking for but I expect you have heard from Pa that the 1912 one is the one I should like to get hold of. It is the result of an argument, in which one of the chaps in our platoon claims to have played in the County team. The pork pie arrived all serene and was enjoyed very much by me. Yes! the Russians appear to be giving the Austrians socks and I sincerely hope they will keep on doing so. Am glad to hear you are all keeping fairly fit, and am glad to say I am the same. Of course Reg is quite used to the Egyptian heat, so he will not be affected so much as his comrades. Will dry up now.
With best love to all, Yrs ever, Pud.

On the 19th June 1916 Ray's Company went back to dug–outs at Carnoy and worked under 79th Company, Royal Engineers. The rest of the battalion joined on the 24th and the 10th Essex prepared to take part in the British offensive which was to yield the greatest number of casualties in one single day in the history of warfare up until this time – what we now know as the Battle of the Somme.

The build up is described here as published in 'The Essex Regiment 10th Battalion' which in turn has been taken from the War Diary.

The Essex Regiment 10th Battalion

On June 22nd general and special instructions were issued to companies and the next day the first operation order followed. The brief record of the remaining days of June until the memorable July 1st runs:–

"U" Day (June24th). Bombardment by heavy guns commenced. Enemy made practically no reply, only firing a few H.E. shrapnel (15cm.) between 10p.m. and midnight. Our 2in. T.M. also very active against the enemy's wire. Headquarters moved from Bray to A1 Headquarters, Carnoy. Company work continued under 79th Coy. R.E., chiefly digging of Lapree Avenue.

"V" Day (June25th). Bombardment continued. 2in. T.M. extremely active. During the afternoon two hostile observation balloons were brought down on our front by incendiary bombs dropped from aeroplanes. Aeroplanes also co-operated with the artillery during the afternoon and evening.

"W" Day (June 26th) Bombardment continued 2 ins. T.M. extremely active in early morning. Smoke used during heavy bombardment, which lasted from 9a.m. to 10 a.m. Corps on our left used gas at 11-30 a.m. (reported later as very successful). At dusk the Battalion was relieved by the 8th Norfolk. On relief the Battalion went via Sheffield Avenue to Billon Wood.

"X" Day (June 27th) Bombardment continued. Conference of company commanders held at 12 noon and 9–30p.m. All final details for "move up" on evening of "Y" day arranged and orders issued. (On this day too, men were interested watching French gunners in the wood firing howitzers which had been constructed in 1872 and of which they made very effective use).

"Y" Day (June 28th) Bombardment continued. Advanced parties moved forward in accordance with programme at 12–15p.m. Brigade informed us that all infantry operations were suspended for 48 hrs. The bombardment continued just the same. The enemy fired on Billon Wood with a mixed variety of shells during the evening and night.

June 29th was the day originally fixed for the assault, but it was postponed for 48hrs. hence the following record.

"X" Day again (June 29th) Bombardment continued. Enemy shelled Billon Wood slightly during the evening, first with lachrymatory, later with shrapnel. Two men wounded.

"Y" Day again (June 30th) Bombardment continued. Advance parties sent into Carnoy in morning. Battalion moved up during evening and established itself in the trenches of the Carnoy defences.

Ray managed a short letter on the 30th describing forthcoming events with massive understatement as a "sporting event".

17812   30–6–16
Dear Hal,
Thanks very much for the Norfolk Football Annual and letter, the 1912 one was the right one. Those tablets are O.K. and suit me just as well as the others. We are having a lot of excitement out here and expect to have more in the days to come. Have just seen some of our Aeroplanes bring down a German, it was quite an interesting sight as well as gratifying. I am just about to partake in a sporting event of which you may hear about later. Well Hal news is scarce so you must excuse this short note. Hoping you are all serene, as it leaves me at present. Love to all,
Yrs. ever, Pud.

The 10th Essex looked out across this landscape towards their objectives for the day. This is, as far as can be determined, the point from which Ray and his fellow-soldiers climbed from their trench.

ADVANCE ON THE SOMME

Whilst the letters illustrate that the men of the ranks were aware that a great attack was imminent they probably had little concept of the enormity of the enterprise. The main Allied attack of 1916 was originally planned for August but brought forward to relieve the pressure on the French line further south at Verdun, It took place on a 30 kilometre front from north of the river Somme between the towns of Arras and Albert.

The bombardment by 1,500 guns began on 24th June; on July 1st 750,000 Allied troops, the greater part of them British, took part in the advance. At the end of the first day 58,000 were lost, about one third of them being killed. Ray was in one of the very few elements of the advancing forces which actually achieved its objectives on 1st July; the attacks continued into November and even then some targets for Day One had only just been achieved.

 To give a full account of this memorable day and those that followed is not the brief of this book but I try to give here an impression of what it was like from contemporary accounts and, of course, Ray's letters. It must be remembered that the 10th Essex was part of the 53rd Brigade which in turn was part of the 18th Division.

The 18th Division was one of the few that attained all its objectives on July 1st. It was part of the XIII Corps serving with the Fourth Army (Rawlinson) and it advanced 3,000 yds. on a front of 2,500 yds., seized Montauban Ridge and the west end of Montauban village and captured Pommiers Redoubt.

Extracts from Operational Order No.1 issued by Lt. Col. H.L. Scott commanding 10th(S) Battalion Essex Regiment.

23rd June 1916.
Information 1. The 53rd Inf. Bde. will take part in the attack on the German trenches. The front allotted the Bde. is from junction of BATTY ROAD and front trenches (exclusive) to junction of YORK ROAD and trench A7/2 (inclusive) — 650x. The 55th Inf. Bde. is on our right: the 54th Inf. Bde. is on our left.

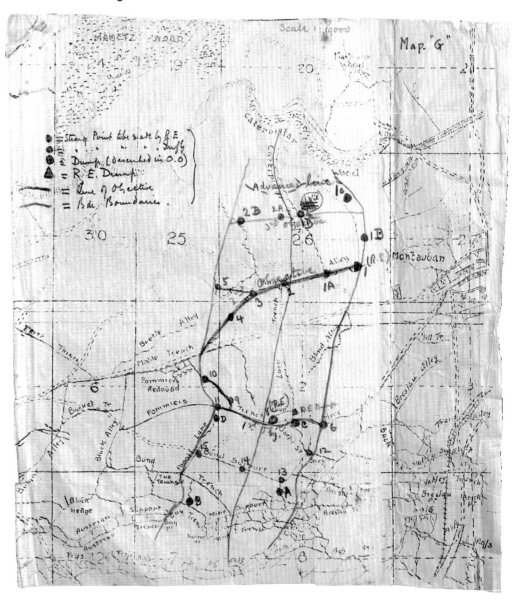

Information 2. The 10th Essex Regt. will be support ("C") Bn. of the Bde. –The 8th Norfolk Regt. and the 6th R. Berks. Regt. will be right and left front Battalions respectively. 8th Suffolk Regt. is the Reserve ("D") Bn.

Objective 3.(b) of 10th Essex Regt. POMMIER TRENCH from Pt. A2d.22.58 (inclusive) to junction with POPOFF LANE, (inclusive) – The LOOP–POMMIERS LANE from junction with POMMIER TRENCH to Pt. A1b.85.15 (inclusive).

Main Task 5. The main task of the 10th Essex Regiment is to consolidate and hold at all costs its objective as shown in Para.3. The Pommier Trench line is to be held at all costs even if MAMETZ and MONTAUBAN are not taken.

Principles of Attack 7. These are as laid down in Fourth Army Tactical Notes –May 1916.
N.B. Once the objectives have been gained troops must dig and work hard to strengthen them against inevitable counter attack during the next 48 hours. No Battn. will be relieved until it has completed the consolidation set it.

Ray wrote in his diary.

The eve of the attack June 30th very heavy bombardment. July 1st: The attack starts at 7–30a.m., the first wave goes over and No.12 section follows with bombs and ammo., we carry for 48hrs. under heavy shell fire. The 18th Division take four lines of trenches and reaches all its objectives.

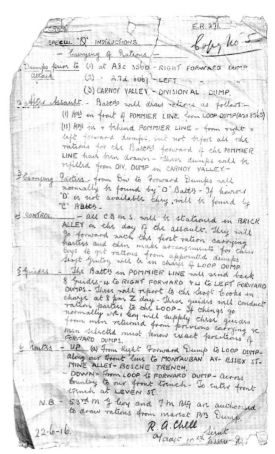

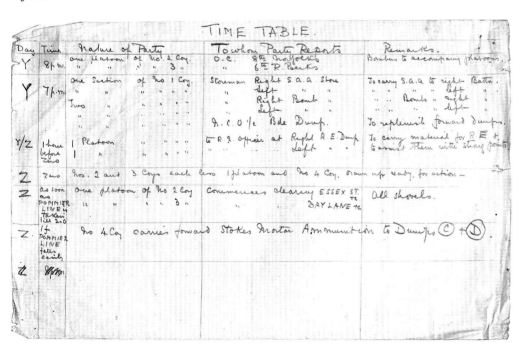

This description was written by the Adjutant Lieut. R.A.Chell.

Part of a Stokes mortar, pictured in Trônes wood, May 2007, with a 10p piece to show scale. The debris of war is still found, nearly a century on.

About 7–20a.m. our hurricane bombardment became a veritable whirlwind. All our lighter artillery and Stokes mortars played to their utmost on the front line and close support trenches of the enemy system. This was the first time Stokes mortars had been used "all–out" and their effect was at least spectacular; the air was full of toppling and turning cylinders at various stages of flight. And yet other noises and excitements were in store for us in that 10 minutes which preceded our zero hour. At 2 minutes to zero our tunnellers blew strongly charged mines below the old minefield on our right front and below "Kasino Point", slightly to our left; sappers simultaneously blew the charges to open the Russian saps they had made in preceding weeks, as communication trenches with the enemy front line. Kasino Point filled the air around us with lumps of chalk of varying sizes, and a fair number of our men were injured by them. Our little shack was on the trench level, and was quite open on the west side. Several hunks came into this den, and the colonel's servant, Hodges, who was standing at the opening, was almost stunned. He suffered badly from concussion for the rest of the day. As soon as the mines went up the assaulting troops went over the top, and halted for a few seconds to get their line straight. The barrage lifted, and forward they all went with cheers and yells straight for the Huns. The line 100 yds. away was invisible for a time – there was so much smoke. ------------- "A" Company was carrying and helping the sappers.

The 1st July was full of tragedy for the majority of British divisions – Regular, Service and Territorial. For us of the 18th Division, who were not blooded before that day, it was a magnificent victory. Countless reasons may be adduced to account for our success. Apart from the courage and efficiency of our officers and men, their wonderful enthusiasm and esprit de brigade, I would emphasise the untiring devotion of our commanders to their respective jobs. Those of us still remaining salute Maxse and Higginson for the training they gave us and the preparations they made for the battle. In every case the soundness of their respective decrees was established.

Ray managed to send a card out on July 4th.

Dear Hal,
I am still alive and kicking although going through H____ itself. We have taken several lines of German trenches and it was hot work while it lasted. This is a card I pinched from a German dugout.
With love to all, Yrs. ever, Pud.
P.S. Sergt. Jefferies is wounded.

Ray wrote in his diary,

Caterpillar Wood is captured by "D" and "C" Companies of the Essex Regiment and 1 field gun, July 4th 1916. We have now held the captured trenches for four days and been spending all the time in burying dead Huns.

The Battalion went into support on the rainy night of July 4th – 5th which prevented the removal of guns as souvenirs, with "A" and "C" Companies holding Mine Alley, Back Trench and Breslau, and "B" and "D" in the old front line in the rear. Their duty was to be ready to turn out at a moment's notice in support of the 8th Suffolk in Montauban Alley.

Letters followed on the 6th.

17812
Dear Pa, Ma, and Syb,
Thanks very much for your letters. I am glad to say I am all serene after my little escapade over the parapet. I have just received a letter from Theo, who says he is trying to see Reg. I expect you have had an anxious time wondering how I have been progressing and am glad to say I have pulled through all serene although at times I didn't expect to. Well we are still holding the Huns in our new trenches and although they tried a counter attack, they didn't move us. I am writing this letter in a Hun dug–out which is 30ft. under the ground and withstood our heavy bombardment. Do you know Ma, I could have eaten two or three of your chickens, just after we got into the German lines. Well dear people have put most of the news in Hal's letter so you must excuse this being short.
Hoping you are all in the pink, With best love to all, From Raymond.

It does not seem inappropriate to include here the two cards which Ray evidently picked up and kept whilst in these formerly enemy trenches – cards from home to a young soldier, Herman Koch.

Musketeer Herman Koch
1st Company
26th Infantry Regiment
Fieldpost 7
Infantry Divsion
Western Front

Ll. Wanzleben   21.5.16
BZ Magdeburgh
Dear Brother,
This is to let you know that we have received your leter today midday. We are all still in good health. I send you herewith a card which is from me and Selma.
Greetings, Hermina, Mother, Selma and Grandma.

Gr. Ottrleben   14.2.1916
Bz Magdeburg

Dear Herman,
We were pleased on receiving your card. Don't be upset that Otto with our father made calves' sweetbread broth at the Strumpfs. We hope you will soon be having leave and father will be making broth with you there as well. We are looking forward to that. We'd also like

to tell you that Walter has also been called up on 11.2.16. He is here in Friedrichstadt and has first to be trained. Hopefully the war will be over soon. Everyone here is all right and we hope that you are fine too.
Lots of love, the Goedek familly and Walter Siebst.
Parcel will be sent to you on 14th February.

The letter to Hal, written from the captured German trenches, gives Ray's account of July 1st. When parts of the letter became public knowledge locally, it caused quite a stir and was the source of some embarrassment to the young soldier.

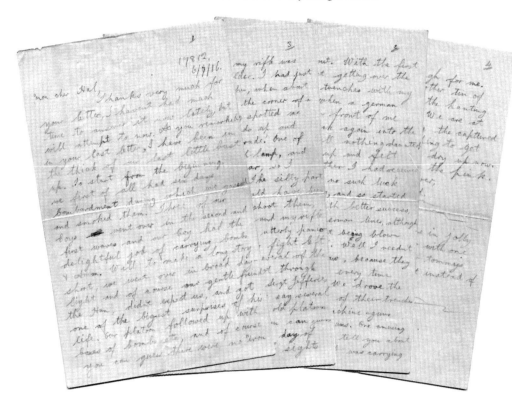

17812 6–7–16
Mon Cher Hal,
Thanks very much for your letter, I haven't had much time to answer it now lately, but will attempt to now. As you remarked in your last letter, I have been in the thick of our last little bust up. To start from the beginning, we first of all had six days bombardment during which we gassed and smoked them. Three of our Coys. went over in the second and first waves and our Coy. had the delightful job of carrying bombs and ammo. Well to make a long story short, we went over in broad daylight and of course our gentle friend the Hun, didn't expect us, and got one of the biggest surprises of his life. Our platoon followed up with boxes of bombs etc., and of course you can guess there were no "iron rations" flying about. With the first load, I was just getting over the parapet of our trenches with my load of bombs, when a German shell burst just in front of me and blew me back again into the trench. Well nothing daunted I picked myself up and felt

around to see whether I had received a "blighty one". But no such luck I found nothing wrong, and so started off again, this time with better success, safely reaching the German lines, although how I did so without being blown to pieces is a marvel. Well I needn't go into the sights I saw, because they make me feel sick every time I think about them. We drove the Huns out of three lines of their trenches and captured several machine guns and one or two field–guns. One amusing little incident I must tell you about which happened while I was carrying two boxes of bombs and my rifle was slung across my shoulder. I had just reached the boche trenches, when about twenty Germans came round the corner of a trench, and directly they spotted me they all put their hands up and yelled "comarade, comarade". One of them gave me a flash–lamp, and another gave me a cigar, so I shouldn't shoot them. The silly part of it was, that it would have been impossible for me to shoot them with the load I had and my rifle slung, but they were so panic stricken that they had no fight left in them. I have seen several of the Norfolk chaps who got through alright, but I hear Sergt. Jefferies is wounded. Am sorry to say several of the chaps out of my old platoon have gone under and you can guess I didn't eat much on the day of the attack, the fearful sights I saw were food enough for me. Could you send another tin of Harrisons Pomade as the hunting season is coming

Lance-Corporal R. Randall.

LANCE-CORPORAL RAYMOND RANDALL, the youngest son of Bro. R. L. Randall, who is Senior District Trustee, the brother himself being a lifelong member of the Order, is now in hospital in Liverpool suffering from shrapnel wounds. He says: "After we had given the Germans six days' bombardment three of our companies went over in the first and second waves, and our company had the delightful job of carrying bombs and ammunition. We went over in broad day-light, and, of course, our gentle friend the Hun did not expect us, and got one of the biggest surprises of his life. Our platoon followed up with bombs, etc., and as I was getting over the parapet of our trenches with my load of bombs a German shell burst right in front of me and blew me back again. I picked myself up, found nothing wrong, and started off once more, safely reaching the German lines, although how I did so without being blown to pieces was a marvel.

LNC.-CPL. RANDALL.

"One amusing little incident happened to me while I was carrying two boxes of bombs, and my rifle was slung across my shoulder. I had just reached the Bosche trenches when about twenty Germans came round the corner of a trench, and directly they spotted me they all put their hands up and yelled 'Camerade.' One of them gave me a flash lamp and another gave me a cigar so that I should not shoot them. The silly part of it was that it would have been impossible for me to shoot them with the load I had and my rifle slung; but they were so utterly panic-stricken that they had no fight left in them"

The story as it appeared later in the Rechabite Friendly Society magazine.

83

on. We are at present still holding the captured trenches and are hoping to get relieved soon. Must dry up now.
Hoping you are in the pink.
Yrs. Ever, Pud.
P.S. Those Horlicks came in jolly useful. Could also do with one of those big refills for tommy's cooker, one a fortnight instead of one every three weeks.

Relief came on the evening of the 7th by the 1st Royal Scots Fusiliers, and was completed in good time, notwithstanding the traffic congestion on the muddy Carnoy roads. The cheery Battalion spent the night at Bonfray Farm and on July 8th moved to the new and comfortable camp known as Grovetown, at Bray, where a small draft was received. Colonel Scott, on 9th July, complimented all ranks upon what had been achieved and read the congratulatory messages, whilst, by the aid of maps, the communiqués were explained, so that the Battalion should understand the part which had been played.

The next letter was written from Grovetown before Ray went back into action on the 13th–14th July.

17812   11–7–16
Dear Hal,
Thanks very much for your letter, I expect you will have received my other letter by now in which I described my experiences in going over the top. We are now resting at the back of the lines, after having been relieved, by another Div., from the trenches we took. I think I mentioned in the last letter, that I had received your last parcel, for which many thanks. I am sorry to say that young Allen of the Norfolks ("Loady"), has been knocked out, I saw him last in the German lines and spoke to him just before he went under. I haven't heard yet how the other Cromer chaps got on, but have seen Jack Blythe's brother and Sergt. Gray. I have collected several souvenirs but of course whether I shall get them home is a question. The Germans had several types of bayonets and I saw one or two of the saw–edge variety. Have just been down to the river for a bathe and I enjoyed it very much. Oh! by the way, could you send me another one of those belts for insects as the German dug–outs which I have been sleeping in lately were rather lively. Well Hal I think this is all just now.
With much love to all, Yrs. ever, Pud.

A further extract from Ray's diary:

July 13th March up again to Billon Wood. July 14th at 2–30a.m. 3rd Div. and 9th go over the top and gain more ground, we shift up to Trônes Wood which we capture and fortify, German shell us heavily and counter–attack but are repulsed and lose heavily many blightees. On July 15th the enemy again shell heavily to cover the retirement of their guns. Relieved on July 16th by the 35th Div.(Bantams) and shift back to Billon Wood.

Corporal Fred Allen shares his grave with Private Laurens of the Manchester Regiment. They lie in Carnoy cemetery, just behind the lines from where the Norfolks and the 10th Essex advanced.

Trônes Wood, a narrow triangle of woodland, seems today like any other wood - until you check against the trench map and realise you're standing in the remains of the long trench that ran down the side of the wood, where men fought and died.

The 53rd Infantry Brigade was first for action, and of that brigade the 10th Essex would go first. As they moved off at dawn on the 14th July 1916 the skies to the east and north–east were ablaze with gun flashes and alarm signals, the roads beside our camp were thronged with Indian cavalry moving forward to uncertain tasks, and amongst it we moved off as the van of the 53rd Brigade.

With the 10th Essex in France

This photograph of Trônes Wood from the "Michelin Guide to the Battlefields of the Somme", first published in 1919, illustrates the extent to which the woodland was destroyed by artillery fire.

85

The 9th Division had attacked on the right that morning, and the South African troops had taken the greater part of Delville Wood [only to be driven out again later]. Our job was to hold a line covering their flank. British troops already held Trones Wood, and so our dispositions were Trones Alley (a trench running from the N.E. of Bernafay Wood to the N. apex of Trônes Wood), and the eastern edge of Bernafay. "A" and "D" Companies held these lines, and "B" and "C" Companies were in reserve in Bernafay Wood.

The Essex Regiment 10th Battalion

Dead lay thickly round about Longueval Alley and stretcher bearers were busy the whole night long [July 13th/14th]. The Battalion – which had two companies in Trones Alley and the eastern edge of Bernafay Wood and two in reserve in Bernafay Wood – expected orders to attack at any moment, but it was not until 5–30p.m. that information came that it would not be required. Shelling was considerable and the Battalion headquarters received five direct hits, though without dire results. "A" Company were the worst sufferers in Trones Alley; in all some eighty officers and men were killed and wounded in forty–eight hours.

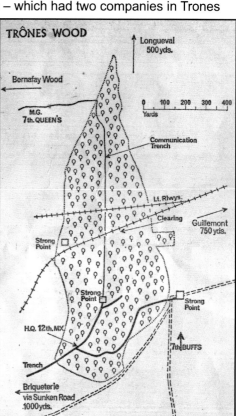

"A" Company certainly had a rough time. The shelling was vile.

Relief came on the evening of the 16th, and the Battalion trudged back to Billon Wood for what was a short–lived rest.

There is one letter which Ray managed to write on the 14th, 15th and 16th July which reflects in some small way what he and his comrades must have been going through in those 48 hours.

17812   14–7–16
Dear Pa, Ma, and Syb,
Thank awfully for your letters. I am just off to the line again to drive the nasty Hun a little further back. I expect you will have received my other letters by this, in which I gave a graphic description of my experiences.

15–7–16
We are once again in the line, the Div. which relieved us last time, went over the top this morning and pushed the boches still further back. We are now holding a trench and wood, out of which the Huns had to get, and have been shelled nearly all the time we have been in, but you can bet we shall hang on. I have received all parcels up to time of writing, received last one today and many thanks for the good things contained. The "Tommies Cooker" is extra useful this week as we can only get dry stuff up where we are. The Huns are buzzing shells over all the time I am writing this, and several of my

comrades have received "blighty wounds" but so far I am intact.

16–7–16
We have been relieved today and have now shifted to just behind the lines again, I think
I should have gone potty if we had stopped there much longer. I expect I shall get a
chance to post this today as they haven't taken any letters in since we went up the line.
Well dear people will close now with best love to everyone.
Yrs. Affect. Raymond. xxxxxx
P.S. Could you send me another razor as have smashed my other one.

The next letter shows how Ray had become increasingly hardened to the horrors of war.
It is the last letter he wrote from France. At 7p.m. on the day the letter was written the
Battalion moved off at short notice to a battle that was to leave many of their number
killed or wounded, including Ray and his pal Albert Wheeler.

17812   18–7–16
Dear Hal,
Thanks very much for your letter. I have written several letters and expect you will have
received them by now. We are now having a short rest again after being under heavy
shell fire for three days in which we had a good many casualties. Expect to be going
over the top again shortly and of course as the "Jocks" say, "with the best of luck". I
have received every parcel so far and hope I shall have the same luck with the others. I
am just getting used to this game of war, and the sights which at first made me feel sick,
I now don't take any notice of. The Huns still keep giving themselves up and they don't
half look pleased with themselves when they find they are in our lines. Well Hal haven't
time to write much, so will close.
Hoping you are all serene, Love to all, Yrs. ever, Pud.

So far the 53rd Brigade had not suffered heavily in the Somme struggle, but it was
soon to be taxed to the utmost in perhaps the most stubborn wood fighting of military
history, that of Delville Wood.

The Essex Regiment
10th Battalion

At 7p.m. [on the 18th July] the Brigade moved to Bois de Talus and three hours later
the Battalion had settled down in Carnoy Valley, opposite Bois de Talus, in comfortless
shelters. Early on the morning of the 19th urgent orders came for the Essex to proceed
to the Brigade rendezvous in Caterpillar Valley whilst Colonel Scott rode to Maricourt
for orders. By 3–30a.m. the Battalion lay in artillery formation on the right of the
Montauban–Longueval road near to Bernafay Wood, and an hour and a half later the
commanding officer returned with the news that the 53rd Brigade had been lent to the
9th Division to retake Longueval and Delville Wood. The latter was roughly rectangular
in shape, divided into more or less equal parts by a ride which ran east to west from
Longueval and which was known as Princes Street. Another ride in the south side of
the wood was named South Street. The wood, with the exception of the south–western
corner and part of Longueval, had been recaptured by the enemy as the result of a heavy
counter–attack. The general idea was that the 8th Norfolk should clear the wood south of
Princes Street and that the Essex and Berkshires, who had followed in the wake, should
clear the northern portion of the wood whilst the 8th Suffolk retook Longueval village

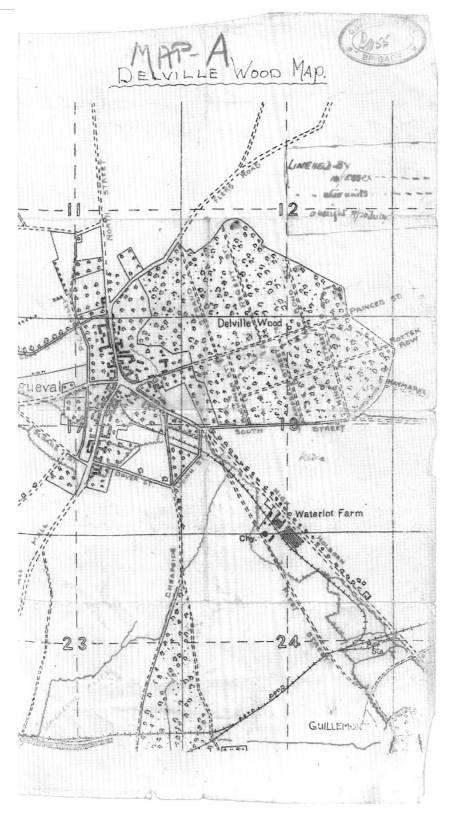

The detailed orders for the 10th Essex were that they should follow the 8th Norfolk and move forward an hour and a half after the latter's operation had commenced. The right of the Battalion would be on the eastern edge of the wood and left on Regent Street, the 6th Royal Berkshire taking up the remainder of the line on that flank. "A"and"D" Companies were in the Battalion's front line, the latter with the eastern edge of the wood to Bond Street as their objective and "A" Company from Bond Street to Regent Street.

The first company of the Norfolks left at 5–20a.m. and the first company of the Essex moved off at 5–45a.m. Up to this time no casualties had been suffered, because the German shellfire fell 180 yds. short. The move along the Montauban–Longueval road was very slow and had died down before the rear company of the Essex had started. The road was in a very bad state, cumbered with dead and wounded and littered with the debris of war. The Brigade had to move more or less in single file all the way. The most pertinent reason for the slow progress, however, was the fact that there was only one entrance into the wood on the south side and that was under direct machine gun fire, so that the Norfolks, who had put three companies into the wood, had difficulty in working forward, though by hard fighting they managed to clear it to Princes Street and get as far east as Buchanan Street.

By 10–30a.m. the Essex were aware that all the Norfolks were in the wood, but were held up between Campbell Street and King Street and required support. Forty minutes afterwards two platoons of "A" Company were in action assisting the left flank of the Norfolks.

"A" and "D" Companies were ordered to get into position as soon as

88

possible, but not to advance north of Princes Street until the order was given. This was accomplished shortly after noon, but there was some difficulty in obtaining touch; in fact, communication with the 6th Royal Berkshire was not secured until about 3p.m. Half an hour afterwards three efforts were successively made to move forward from the Princes Street line, but the hostile machine gun fire was too tenacious and our own heavy artillery had not lifted sufficiently.

The inevitable was recognized at 5–10p.m. when orders came to consolidate on the line and to hold tightly thereto. By 6–15p.m. the company dispositions were known. The four companies were in front, under the immediate command of Captain Tween, with the Norfolks on the right facing east and the Berkshires on the left, in a south–westerly direction. A strong point was pushed out from the Essex and held by a corporal and ten men with a Lewis gun. The left was bent back so as to form a defensive flank towards Longueval, for the enemy were very active north of the village and in the north–eastern corner of the wood. A platoon of about forty men was stationed in the wood south of Rotten Row between Campbell Street and King Street for the purpose of counter–attack. The front line was held by about 250 men, with two Vickers guns and eight Lewis guns, the greater portion of which were so situated that they could fire along the northern front.

It was during this day, the 19th July 1916, that Ray received his "Blighty" wound. His diary reads:

Up the line again on July 18th to Delville Wood and make an attack on it. Wounded in Delville Wood on the 19th '16 in right leg, admitted to No. 6 General Hos. on 21st July 1916. Operated on 22nd '16. Moved from Rouen on 25–7–16 to Blighty. Landed at Southampton on 26–7–16. From there to Highfield Military Hospital, Knotty Ash L'pool. Operated on again on 23rd Aug. '16 Highfield Military Hospital. Transferred from there to Colne House R.C.H. Cromer Nfk. June 2nd 1917.

Delville Wood is today the main South African memorial recalling that nation's participation in the First World War. The carefully tended lawns and the memorial buildings command respect whilst the broad 'streets' through the wood carry the same names as in 1916. The 10th Essex and the Norfolks desperately tried to hold this south-east corner; somewhere near here, amongst the then shattered tree-stumps, Ray was wounded and lay for many hours.

These few bland statements give no idea of the bitterness and horror of the fighting that took place in Delville Wood and decimated the 10th Essex Regiment, indeed the whole of the 53rd Brigade. Neither does it convey the long struggle Ray had in coping with his leg wound. It was to be a reminder to Ray for the rest of his life. Only his close family knew that the wound had to be continually re–dressed to the day he died in 1977, to prevent it causing the loss of his leg.

BACK TO BLIGHTY

Ray managed to send a Field Postcard dated 23–7–16 and postmarked 27–7–16 from France. He sent a postcard from Highfield Hospital Liverpool, postmarked 27–7–16 Liverpool.

Dear Pa,
I am now in Blighty with a small shrapnel wound in the right leg. Am at hospital in Liverpool and landed in Southampton this morning. Will write with more news later. Yours affectionately, Raymond.

Ray wrote a letter on the 27th July.

17812   Highfield Military Hosp., Knotty Ash, Liverpool. 27–7–16
Dear Pa,
At last I am able to write a letter to you to let you know how I am progressing. I am getting on finely and have been lucky enough to get into this hospital, it's absolutely another "Colne House", the only disadvantage being so far from home. We were attacking a wood called "Delville Wood", when the piece of shell took a fancy to my leg and hand, but you can see by this letter that there's not much wrong with my hand. God was very good to me in the case of my leg, as the piece of shell just grazed the bone and only laid open the mussel (sic). Of course it's rather a large wound but is quite clean and with the good treatment I am receiving here, will soon be well. I underwent an operation at Rouen, and was in the hospital there two days. I was also very fortunate with my hand, the piece of shrapnel grazed the tissues which control the working of my thumb. Well Pa hope all are well at home, and please don't worry about me as am now

HIGHFIELD MILITARY HOSPITAL, LIVERPOOL.   HIGHFIELD MILITARY HOSPITAL, LIVERPOOL. (A NURSING PAVILION)

in capable hands.
With best love to all, From your loving son, Raymond.
P.S. Could you send another writing pad as lost all my kit in the wood.

Following are three letters all written on 1st August.

"C" Block 17812, Highfield Military Hospital, Knotty Ash, Liverpool   1–7–16
Dear Pa and Ma,
Thanks very much for your letter which I have just read. My leg is a bit more painful today, as they have put it in a splint, and there is a crack in the bone. Am still having hot formalin on it to clean it and the wound itself is looking very well. You got rather mixed Pa, as to the dates in your last letter. I was wounded on the 19th, arrived at Rouen on the 21st, operated on, on the 22nd, left Rouen on the 25th, arrived in England on the 26th and also at Liverpool. Yes! I received your telegram (for which many thanks) on Saturday. Thanks very much Ma for the writing paper, envelopes etc., they have proved very useful. Young Jordan got wounded just before me on the same day, while he was bandaging one of the chaps up. It was very fortunate for me, that I knew how to stop the bleeding in my leg, as I might easily have lost my life, as all our stretcher–bearers were knocked out, and had to manage it myself and a couple of my chums found up a stretcher and carried me about two miles to the dressing station. I was wondering all the time whether I should get another "blighty" as the shells were falling fast and furious. Have just had a letter from Wilf. He appears to be enjoying himself, his other letter was also interesting. Well Ma am sorry you sent the chicken, but I think it will find a home, as I told my chums to open all parcels sent out rather than send them back. Oh Pa, if the razor happens to come back, could do with it and also a shaving brush, as the barber only visits about once a week. I feel in health absolutely fit, but the wounds are jolly painful especially when being dressed. Well Pa and Ma will conclude now.
With best love to all,
from your loving son, Raymond. xxxxx

"C" Block 17812, Highfield Military Hospital, Knotty Ash, Liverpool. 1–8–16
Dear Wilf,
Was very pleased to receive your letter. It is not a serious wound although a large one and expect it will be some time before I can get onto my feet. I got it in Delville Wood on the second day of our attack, I was taking cover in a shell hole when a piece of a bally whizz–bang caught me in the right leg, but fortunately only cracked the bone instead of fracturing it. They have sent me your interesting letter of your tour and have enjoyed reading it. Yes, I shall get leave when I am discharged from here, but expect it will be several weeks yet. I should like to have been with you hunting those Zepps. I should think it was very exciting. Well Wilf, will dry up now, hoping you are in the pink.
With best wishes, Yrs. Ever, Pud.

"C" Block   17812   1–8–16
Dear Hal,
Thanks ever so much for your welcome letter. They have just put my leg in a splint and

92

it isn't half giving me beans, they have found that the bone is cracked but it's nothing serious. I'm glad they captured that wood at last, but at what cost, our Brigade was almost wiped out when I left after only two days of fighting. I think that wood and village fighting is absolutely murder, the Germans had a machine gun behind every tree in Delville Wood and it was just like charging a brick wall. The Rev. Gethen has

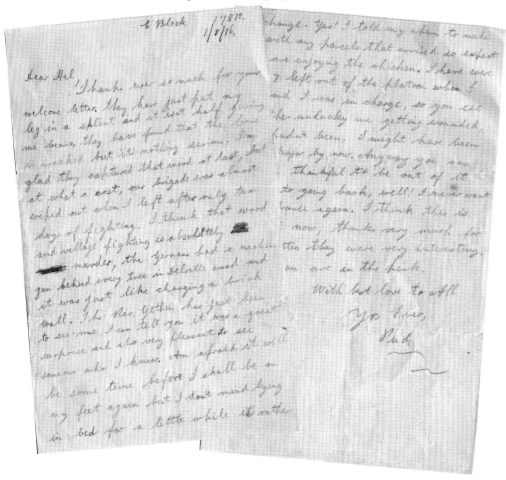

just been to see me, I can tell you it was a great surprise and also very pleasant to see someone who I knew. Am afraid it will be some time before I shall be on my feet again but don't mind lying in bed for a little while it's rather a change. Yes! I told my chums to make of with my parcels that arrived so expect they are enjoying the chicken. There were only 7 left out of the platoon when I left and I was in charge, so you see it's rather unlucky me getting wounded, if I hadn't been, I might have been Sergt. Major by now. Anyway you can bet I'm thankful to be out of it and as to going back, well! I never want to see France again. I think this is all just now, thanks very much for Reg's letters they are very interesting. Hoping you are in the pink.
With best love to all, Yrs. Ever, Pud.

I have included here a letter to Ray's father from the Rev. Gethen who had visited Ray in hospital.

From; The Rev.L.Gethen M.A., St. Mark's Vicarage, Edgeley Road, Stockport
August 1st 1916
Dear Mr Randall,
I went to Liverpool yesterday and found Raymond. He has a nasty hole in the muscle of his right calf and probably won't walk for a bit but he is very well otherwise and very happy and cheerful. He says he is very comfortable and well looked after. The Hospital is a very nice one and beautifully situated in grounds and everything seems to be done for the patients. I saw him eat a very good dinner and had an hours chat with him and when I came away he said my visit had quite cheered him up. He was very surprised to see me. You need not worry about him at all, he will probably be about in a few weeks and I should think he has every prospect of a perfect recovery and no ill effects in the future. He is not at all sorry to have left the fighting and to be safe in England again – no wonder. I wish he was nearer to me as I am unfortunately too busy to go so far again to see him at present, but please let me know if there is anything I can do at any time, and if at anytime you get anxious and think he is not getting on I will gladly make time to go to him. I know how you will thank our Heavenly Father for his goodness.
With kindest regards, Yours very sincerely,
L.Gethen.

As Ray began his long road to recovery in hospital, the fight for Delville Wood continued. Although we can't be sure, it is possible that Ray lay wounded for over 24 hours before he was removed to an aid station. As he said himself, his St John Ambulance training enabled him to know that he must apply a tourniquet to his leg.

The Essex Regiment 10th Battalion

The casualties for the series of operations had been severe, particularly on the night of the 19th–20th July, 4 officers were killed and 19 wounded. Of other ranks 75 were killed (including Ray's pal Albert Wheeler, killed on 20th July), 38 were missing and 402 were wounded.

I do not propose to give a long and heartrending account of those two dreadful days in Delville Wood – they were certainly the most trying days I myself have ever experienced.

The other battalions lost as heavily as we did. Everyone found the place nerve–racking; the senior company commander and the adjutant of another battalion were sent down complete nervous wrecks. For a long time it continued to be difficult to get wounded away, but things became a bit quieter in the late afternoon, and certain bearer parties of dismounted cavalry came up to help our stretcher bearers.

The night of 19th–20th was somewhat noisy, and a noisy night in a wood is not at all restful. Isolated Huns, both in Longueval and the Wood, put up streams of multicoloured lights and so gave us a veritable Brock's benefit. Here and there little scraps took place and at one stage of the night the enemy threatened to rush our headquarters.

On the morning of the 20th other troops were hurried into the Wood to continue the attack.

Almost a month passed before Delville Wood was completely cleared of the enemy. Our men were wonderful. The majority of all ranks who went into Delville Wood were "original" 10th Essex. It was a very meagre skeleton that came out.

The 53rd Infantry Brigades counterattack on Delville Wood was the most miserable and at the same time most costly operation in which the Battalion took part during the time I was serving with it, and I believe no one will contradict me if I say that the Battalion never again played a part in any battle anything like so unsatisfactory as this one.

Ray continued to write regularly from his hospital bed. Although many of the letters concern general family chatter there are several interesting and informative sections featuring, amongst other things, the injury, tanks, and other Norfolk soldiers, so they are published here with only limited editing.

C Block., 17812 L'pool 10–8–16
Dear Hal,
Thanks very much for your letter, you must have been thinking of Reg. when you wrote the last letter because you addressed me as dear Reg. I'm awfully sorry you have the "fed up" feeling, you know it's through slogging it too much, I wish my blinking leg was better and that they would give me about a months furlough, then I could come and help you. My leg is a lot less painful now and hurts most when they dress it, it has to be washed out every time then they burrow into it and take the packing out, of course I lays low and says nothing, "I don't think." Yes! I received last weeks parcel all serene and managed to wolf the good things contained therein. I have been on full diet all the time I've been here, I've never felt really ill, it's the pain of my leg. I should very much like to read your "Motorcycling" it will refresh my memory somewhat. The other parcel just arrived, and what a splendid little razor it is, it cuts beautifully, shall have to square you up for the outfit when I come home, please thank everyone for the good things in the parcel. I don't think you can better the contents of the parcels they are "tray–bon." Could you enclose a tooth–brush in the next one as I should like to clean my teeth again. I knew Mr Gee had to go when I was on leave last time, but didn't know he'd gone. I'm awfully sorry for that chap whose thigh is smashed, and here's me grumbling because I've been in bed a fortnight. Well Hal will dry up for the present.
With best love to all, Yrs. ever, Pud.

15–8–16
Dear Pa and Ma,
Thanks very much for your letters. Thank you very much Ma, for putting our photos in, I think they came out very well for press photos, and thanks also for putting my little yarn in, it's a bit of a swank though. Well Pa my leg is swinging along, have started dry dressings now and my word when they pull them off, it doesn't half give me beans. Just imagine pulling off a dressing which is stuck to five square inches of raw flesh and they don't even soak it. The hole round the bone is still discharging and still has to be packed and washed out. My temperature has taken a turn for the better and last night it only went up to 100 degrees, which is quite good, as it kept at 102 degrees for over a week. Must close now.
With best love to all, from your loving son. Raymond. xxxxxxxxxxxxxxxxxxxx

The local newspaper at home recorded Ray's injury and picked up on the story of the enemy troops that had surrendered to him on 1st July.

95

'C' Block 17812, L'pool   16–8–16
Dear Hal,

Thanks ever so much for letter and also for the toothbrush and paste. My leg is looking much better and doesn't sniff like it used to, and my hand is nearly healed. Thanks muchly for the "Motorcycles". I find them very interesting, I say what you think of the "paraffin vaporizer" do you think it will work? Some swank those photos in the "Post" but not at all bad, but it takes the biscuit putting that letter of mine in....Could you send me a few stamps as I am absolutely stony and shan't get any oof till I get out of hospital, I shall have to square you up then. Well I can't think of anything else to talk about except the weather so will dry up. Hoping you are in the pink.
With best love to all, Yrs.Ever, Pud.

"C" Block 17812, L'pool   22–8–16
Dear Hal,

Thanks awfully for the stamps and oof. I didn't really want the oof as I shan't be up just yet, still it will come in useful later so please thank Pa for it..... I expect I shall have to go under another operation shortly, to have the bit of bone taken out, which is driven into the inside of my leg bone, but don't expect it will be a very big job. Have just heard that I go under the operation on Wednesday (tomorrow), so shall have been under it by the time you receive this. Yes! I get plenty in the reading line and they have entertainment every Thursday, but of course I can't go yet, as they won't let me move. I say! That was a bit off, the piece in the "Evening News" the headline said "Cromer lad captures 20 Germans", as I really didn't capture them, they gave themselves up, the piece in the "Post" wasn't so bad, but I would have not had any of them in.... The weather here is now very funny, it's foggy nearly every morning and quite cold and then towards the afternoons it clears up and the sun condescends to shine.
Well Hal will shut up now.
With best love to all,
Yrs. Ever, Pud.

17812
26–8–16
Dear Pa,

Many thanks for your letter. I'm sorry to hear Reg's Commission has again fallen through, he has had some rotten luck, but I hope he will be successful later on.... You know Dad when this rotten old war is over, Theo and I will have to come home and run the business while you and Hal have a holiday.... I have just discovered what was really wrong with my leg, the doctor called it a "compound cone fracture of the right leg". Well Pa I'm glad to see by the papers, that we have brought two more Zepps. down, and if we keep on like that, we shall soon convince the Germans that the game isn't worth the candle. Hoping you are keeping fairly fit.
With best love, your loving son. Raymond.

"C"Block 17812   29–8–16
Dear Hal,

I have successfully recovered from the operation and my leg seems to be going all right.

They did more than take the small piece of bone from inside my leg, they also made the hole on the outside of the bone about twice as big as it was before. The letter from the Navy was from young Daniels, he discovered I was wounded by the "Post". Charlie Walker was one of my pals when I was in No. 1 Platoon, he was transferred to the miners (R.E.) before I left No.1 Platoon, he lives at Swaffham.... I would like to suggest a change in the parcels, if you don't object, I should like a jar of "Seagers? potted meat" instead of quite so much sweet stuff. I didn't feel very chirpy after the operation, but my leg didn't give me any pain, it was only the effects of the ether. But do you know, they had the sauce to starve me for 24hrs. and gave me some rotten caster oil. Hoping you are still in the pink.
With best love to all, Yrs. ever, Pud.

17812 7–9–16
Dear Hal,
Thanks very much for your letter and for the contributions in the parcel.... Yes! the leg is getting on but still discharges from the hole, so of course the bone doesn't grow very quick.... My leg is still in splints because the bone is very weak with the hole, it would snap as easy as anything if it had a decent punch. I'm glad to hear Theo and Reg. are in the pink and hope they will keep out of any more scrapping. Well Hal old man I hope you won't overdo it and go and knock yourself up, I wish I was at home to help you, it makes me feel wild to have to lay in this rotten bed, when I feel that I could be up and doing something useful.... Must dry up now. Hope you are in the pink.
With best love, Yrs. ever, Pud.

17812 14–9–16
Dear Hal,
Thanks muchly for your letter and parcel. Ma has just visited me and is coming again today, you can bet I was pleased to see her.... Mr and Mrs Kelly are getting up a subscription in connection with the Rechabites to get me a chair so I can wheel myself abart (sic) like, later on. Well Hal like you I have no news, only it happens to be the usual thing with me, so will dry up.
With best love, Yrs. Ever, Pud.

The next letter is particularly interesting for its contemporary description of the "new armoured cars", known better to us as tanks. These were used for the first time on the Somme, soon after Ray was wounded.

17812   21–9–16
Dear Hal,
Thanks muchly for your letter and parcel, which was "tray bon" this week. Please thank Ma for the lemon curd and cheese, they were lovely. We have just had another lot of patients in, from the latest advance on the Somme, and all pretty bad cases.... The leg is still O.K. and nothing else gone wrong with it yet. Yes! aren't the Kellys good, Mrs Kelly makes me a cake nearly every week, and brings me her sons books (the one who was

killed at the front) to read. Well I hope Reg. will soon get his commission, I'm sure he deserves it, after all the disappointments he's had.... The news is still bright in the papers isn't it, what do you think of our new armoured cars? A chap next to me who was in the advance with them has been telling me about them. He said that the Huns eyes nearly came out of their heads when they saw them coming towards them, and that our chaps were splitting themselves with laughing as they went over the top, at the sight of them. He says, they are armed with six machine guns and two pom–poms, also they weigh 27 tons and have an armour plating 3 inches thick. Well Hal must dry up now. With best love to all, Yrs. ever, Pud

17812   29–9–16
Dear Hal,
Thanks muchly for your letter and parcel. The Zepps. last Monday came within 18 miles of Liverpool, so I suppose we shall soon be having them here now. Yes! there's no doubt about the "Tanks" saving the infantry losses and they also help demoralise the enemy. I think it's a rotten shame the way Reg. has been treated with regard to his commission don't you? Of course he would take it well, because that's his way, but all the same it isn't right. What do you think of the new push and the huge haul of prisoners, jolly good isn't it? I am pegging along as usual, the hole in my leg is filling up at the rate of 1 thousand parts of an inch per week, but the flesh part is nearly skinned over. Am glad to hear you are keeping fairly fit, I have just recovered from a bit of a cold myself. Will conclude now.
With best love, Yours ever, Pud.

17812   5–10–16
Dear Pa,
Many thanks for your letter. I am still progressing very nicely but have still to keep in bed. I think we are doing very nicely with the German Zepps. don't you, if they keep losing one every time they come over, they will soon begin to think that it's better to stay at home. Yes! Wilf wrote and told me about the shot their gunners had at the supposed Zepp., it was just like those fatheads to forget to take the pins out.... I was sorry to read of the death of those Cromer chaps I knew them all personally. Well dad , I hope you are keeping fit, it makes me wild lying here in bed, when I feel I could be doing something useful. Will conclude now.
With best love, Your loving son, Raymond.

17812   5–10–16
Dear Hal,
Many thanks for your letter and parcel. Yes! I think we have been doing very well in Zepps., and I think we shall soon put the lid on the Zepp. raiding. I measure the progress of my leg, with my eyes, so you see I don't need a micrometer gauge. I expect you get fed up with letter writing, I know I do! and am now tired of wanting to get up, all I ask is to sleep and eat. Can you place a chunk of soap in the parcel next week, the stuff they use here is putrid. That was "some" job putting the clocks back wasn't it, how did you manage the church clock? The weather here continues to be dull and wet. I don't think

much of L'pool weather. I bet Reg Moulton looks a k'nut[sic] in his uniform, how is Con getting on? Well Hal must conclude now. Hoping you are in the pink.
With best love to all, Yrs. ever, Pud.

17812   10–10–16
Dear Ma and Pa,
Thanks very much for your letter... We have just had another convoy in and of course most of them are pretty badly wounded.... Expect to be getting on to a wheelchair soon... Hope to be going to the concert on Thursday, if I can get into the chair. The hole in my leg is filling up and the doctor said I should be alright again by 1920, and I should think the war will be finished by then. Well Pa they say no news is good news, so as I haven't any news it must be good.
With best love to all, from your loving son, Raymond.

17812   12–10–16
Dear Hal,
Many thanks for your letter. I have just been to the concert on a chair and enjoyed it very much.... I really don't think I need so much stuff in the parcels now, you see it's not like being in France, but please thank the contributors all the same.... Well Hal after ten weeks in this beastly bed, I have been allowed to get into a chair and you can't imagine how pleasant the sensation is, I feel as though I could fly. I still have to have my leg in a splint and kept level, because if I let it down the rotten thing starts bleeding. Must close now.
With best love, Yrs. ever, Pud.

17812   17–10–16
Dear Pa,
Many thanks for your letter, and received braces and soap all serene. It will be a good thing for Cromer if those soldiers are billeted at or around about Cromer won't it! Have had to go to bed again as my leg has been misbehaving itself, but expect to be up again soon..... We have just had another lot of wounded in, all bad cases, one chap had lost both legs and one arm, but he was the most cheerful of the lot.
With best love to all, Your loving son, Raymond.

17812   19–10–16
Dear Hal,
Many thanks for your letter and parcel. I went round the hospital laundry yesterday and saw the "Tarts" at work.... I'm afraid I'm getting an awful worry to you, but shall have to worry you again, this time I want you to send me one of my ties, soft collar with front and back stud and pin, one pair of thin socks and one pair of square–bashing boots, of course I shan't be able to use the boots yet but can keep them by me until I can. You see I left my other boots in Delville Wood and shan't be able to get another pair until I leave the hospital. I keep having that bally letter of mine hurled at me every time I have visitors, it's got into the Rechabite Magazine now.
Well Hal have nothing else to write about now.
With best love to all, Yrs. ever, Pud.

Harold Platt, a fellow soldier at the hospital, with whom Ray struck up a friendship.

The next letter was written by Ray's father but was never delivered (stamped "Present Location Uncertain"). It was returned to sender.

Cromer, Sunday 22nd Oct. 1916
Dear Sir,
Shall be glad to hear how you are getting on? My son, Raymond, is still in 'C' Block, Highfield Military Hospital, Knotty Ash, Liverpool, after 11 weeks in bed he is now allowed to get about in a wheelchair with his injured limb supported flat. I have not seen him since he returned to England but his Mother paid him a visit, he has plenty of visitors and is well treated, in fact, I don't think more could be done for him than is being done, only wish he was nearer home so that we could see him sometimes. How is Raymond's other chum who, with you, helped to carry him from Delville Wood? You will both of you be glad to hear that the Doctor tells Raymond that he will by and by be as strong as ever, so that we hope he will long remember his indebtedness to you. We can never thank his chums for their help too much, you undoubtedly saved his life.
Yours truly, R.L.Randall.

17812   25–10–16
Dear Hal,
Many thanks for your letter, and parcel etc. No! the hospital here only supplies the pants and coats you don't get anything else until just before you are discharged, then you have to go to the Military Depot. about five miles from here and draw your kit.... Am glad to hear the Scottish Brigade has come in, it ought to do Cromer some good, and also liven things up somewhat. I hope to be going to the concert tomorrow, as Daisey Dorma is on the programme, and should like to hear her, I hear she is very good. Do you know I have written that bounder Reg. two or three letters and never had a reply, the last time I heard from him was a week or two before I left England in July 1915 and I never had a line since. Well Hal have no more news now so will close. Hoping you are in the pink. With much love, Yrs. Ever, Pud.

17812   31–10–16
Dear Pa,
Many thanks for your letter. I am still wheeling about in my chair, but am getting fed up, because I want to walk about like other people.... I haven't much to write about except that the weather is rotten so I have to keep in the ward.
With best love, Your loving son, Raymond.

17812   7–11–16
Dear Pa,
Many thanks for your letter.... I worried the Dr. so much that yesterday he let me have my splint off, and am now on my peg–legs. Ye wound is healing up nicely, and the hole is getting smaller, I shall always have a bump on my leg where the break was, because the bone forming material has pushed the skin up, but don't think it will seriously effect the leg. You know I'm really beginning to think I should be just as well in France, anyway there's a little more excitement there.... Well, Pa I think this is all just now, I

think I have told you quite a lot about myself this week.
With best love, Your loving son, Raymond.

17812   8–11–16
Dear Hal,
Thanks muchly for your letter and for the letter from Theo. I have now discarded the splint and taken to crutches, on which I walse (sic) around. That slip is only swank, I knew they would send that, but you needn't send on all the cash, if you let me have ten bob it will be enough, then I can square up when I get home. The idea of not sending it to the soldiers in hospital is that they are afraid of them getting tin hattyfied (sic).... The hole in my leg is gradually getting smaller, but my leg feels awfully funny with the splint off. I didn't get any sleep for the first two nights after, my knee gave me a lot of trouble, I expect it was because of being out straight so long. I'm soon going to have a shot at going into L'pool, it's now about 4 months since I saw anything of Blighty. I didn't think I was so much in credit as they sent, I know I was in debt. when I left France... Well Hal I must end the letter as usual and dry up. Hoping you are feeling fit.
With best love to all, Yrs. Ever, Pud.

17812   12–11–16
Dear Hal,
Many thanks for your letter and boots etc.... I have succeeded in upsetting myself again yet am getting on fine.... I think if we paid attention to all the rumours we heard in the army we should soon go potty. You know I really think I ought to do without parcels now. It's not like being in France you know. Say Hal! is there one of my Essex badges knocking around, if so you might mail it on to me, as I can't get one in L'pool, you can have it back when I come home.... We had a chap peg out on the operating table yesterday, he was only walking out with his wife on Tuesday. Well Hal have nothing else to write about so will close.
With best love to all, Yrs. ever, Pud.

17812   14–11–16
Dear Pa,
Many thanks for the letter, stamps, cash etc., which I received all serene.... I went down to L'pool the other day without the aid of my crutches, and have paid for it since. When I got back my foot had swelled to twice its natural size, and the doctor has ordered me back on the wheeled chair. It's all through the silly ass in the bed next to me, he started opening his mouth too wide, and saying that if the doctor saw my foot I should be put back to bed. Of course the Sister, with her extra sharp ears, heard him, and wanted to have a look at my foot. Then of course the doctor must have a look at it, and he sentenced me to the wheeled chair on which I am now tearing my hair. I couldn't say when I shall be home, I'm afraid I shall be some time yet, the hole in my leg is still three–quarters inch deep. I have never felt better in myself and my temperature has never been above 99 since the operation.... The weather is beastly foggy up here now and still wet.
With best love to all, Your loving son, Raymond.

17812   15–11–16

Dear Hal,

Many thanks for your letter. You will have heard about my being back on the chair and the cause thereof so I will not repeat it. Will you see if you can get me a set of the Essex shoulder badges, I went to several shops in the 'pool but couldn't get them, also I could do with another lump of soap. We are allowed out of hospital every day from 2p.m. to 5–30p.m. and from 2p.m. – 8p.m. in the summer months.... I received a letter from Reg and one from Tommy Parker the other day, I see that Tommy is a Lance–Jack. I'm glad to hear Clementines running fairly well, but expect you don't use it much now on account of petrol. Well Hal shall have to dry up now.

   Hoping you are in the pink, Yrs. ever, Pud.

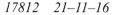

17812   21–11–16

Dear Pa,

Many thanks for your letter.... My foot is down to normal size now and I hope soon to be walking again. I managed to get out on Sunday last again, but of course on the Q.T. and visited Mrs. Kelly's where I had a jolly good time. There may be a chance of my getting home for Xmas, but haven't much hope.... Hoping everyone is feeling fit at home.

From your loving son, Raymond.

17812   24–11–16

Dear Hal,

   Many thanks for your letter. I received the badge etc., also many thanks for the soap.... I pinched out again yesterday and had my photo taken in the town, you see I always get to know when the "sister" is off..... I went over to Birkenhead by tube yesterday, and came back by boat, after I had had my photo taken, there were quite a lot of tarts on the boat. My leg is still getting on slowly, I think the doctors verdict of 1920 is about right. Well Hal I won't allow you to get a pain by reading any more so will conclude.

With best love, Yours Ever, Pud.

The Liverpool photograph.

A card sent from Liverpool to the family at Cromer.

17812   28–11–16

Dear Pa,

Many thanks for your letter and stamps.... Mr. Kelly took me round all the docks and showed me a good bit of L'pool we also inspected a Russian battleship which was just off the quay. I saw young Blythe last, in the first line of German trenches which we had just taken, I was wondering whether he had been bowled over or no. My leg is still getting on nicely, and I am getting about on my feet, after a fashion, but am not supposed to go out yet.... I think this is all now.

With best love to all, Your loving son, Raymond.

17812   29–11–16

Dear Hal,

I am once more upon my own understandings but am not allowed to travel far.... What do you think of the two more Zepps. down, did they do any damage around Norfolk? I managed to pinch out again last Sunday and had a good time at Mrs Kelly's.... Well Hal I'm fed up with being in hospital but I usually get fed up when I've been in particular place any length of time.... Will close now hoping you won't get the pip reading this. With best love to all, Yours Ever, Pud.

17812   5–12–16

Dear Pa,

Many thanks for your letter. I had my letter returned which I wrote to Walter Smith, I believe the Regt. or what was left of them, have been drafted into another Regt. My leg has stopped its swelling tricks but the hole is just the same and little pieces of bone keep working to the surface.... Am glad to hear Theo and Reg. are still all serene. Yes! that was splendid bringing those two Zepps. down. Well Pa have nothing else to write about now.

With best love to all, Your loving son, Raymond.

17812   6–12–16

Dear Hal,

Thanks muchly for your letter and parcel.... I was most unfortunate the other day when I pinched out, I ran right into the sister as I was getting off a tram, so I have to go to bed 'til after lunch now, but I can still get out when the Sister's off..... I'm glad the Zepps. caught a cold again, we are not doing at all badly with them.... I have explored most of L'pool now, but still there are a few things I haven't seen. By the way! the blighters have cut down our leave again, we only get from 2 p.m. to 4 p.m. now. We rushed the rotten old guard the other night, they actually had the sauce to try and stop us from going out. With best love to all, Yours Ever, Pud.

17812   12–12–16

Dear Pa,

Many thanks for your letter. We had a beautiful trench raid last night on the enemy, in the beds across the room. The only thing that spoilt it was the night–nurse came in just as we got up to the enemies wire. Still we didn't stop the raid, so we were reported in the morning and had a lovely lecture.... Have no news just now. With best love to all, Your loving son, Raymond

17812   15–12–16

Dear Hal,

Many thanks for your letter. Once again I expect I shall be for the knife, they are going to scrape the bone this time, it may come off on Saturday, but I am not sure yet. So you see I shall have a Happy Xmas in bed if they perform the operation.... Well Hal haven't anything else to write about now, so think of me on Saturday, somewhat drunk and being knifed. With best love to all, Yours Ever, Pud.

17812
Dear Pa,
Many thanks for your letter and stamps. Have not yet been under my operation, they are going to do it after Xmas, for which I am very thankful.... I can't say who that Cromer lad was, you see there were several of them in the 8th Norfolk in the Delville Wood scrap..... I haven't any more news just now so will close.
With best love, Your loving son, Raymond.

17812 20–12–16
Dear Hal,
Many thanks for your letter and parcel. Please thank everyone for their contributions. They have put off the knifing 'til after Xmas so I shall not be, as expected, namely, in bed... Yes! I think I shall have a little better time this Xmas than last, I don't think I can say that I enjoyed myself. I was surprised to hear that Theo was coming home to take a commission, I shall have to wait patiently for the details. We are at present amusing ourselves by snowballing the nurses and kissing them under the mistletoe, but it's not very exciting. Well Hal I hope you will have a jolly good time this Xmas, and only wish I was at home to share it with you, anyway enjoy yourself and forget all about the bally war. Wishing all at home a Happy Xmas.
 With best love to all, Yours Ever, Pud.

17812   Knotty Ash, L'pool   26–12–16
Dear Pa,
Many thanks for your letter and hope you have all enjoyed yourselves this Xmas. The object of the next operation is to scrape the bone, which when finished will allow the hole in my leg to heal up, and they think there won't be much chance of it breaking down again.... must close now.
With best love, Your loving son, Raymond.

The postcard below is from eldest brother Wilf who visited just before Christmas and wrote to report back to their father. Wilf is the soldier on the right of the postcard picture.

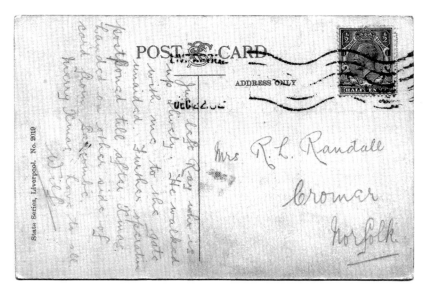

104

17812   29–12–16

Dear Hal,

Very many thanks for your letter. I am still waiting for the operation, I have managed to dodge it until the New Year. I am enclosing a piece of my Tibia, which they fished out of my leg this morning. Of course there are quite a lot of uses to which it can be put, for instance it ought to make a fine stew, or you could wear it as a tie pin... I'm glad Theo isn't getting his commission in a bally infantry Regt., he will be all serene in the R.E.s. Well Hal I had a fairly decent time this Xmas, but I felt all the time that I would rather have been at home. I will close now wishing all at home a very Happy New Year and may all Germans in the next month or two, be frizzling in that hot place.
With best love, Yours Ever, Pud.
P.S. Don't lose that bit of my Tibia.

17812 L'pool 4–1–17

Dear Hal,

Very many thanks for your letter. It is very naughty of Syb. to refuse to make a stew of my tibia, I wonder if she knows there's a war on.... My operation is still on the back list it might come off on Saturday, I wish they would be quick and get it over. I'm glad to hear Reg. is doing all right, and hope he'll soon get his full rank, because acting rank, is not worth anything, I was acting Sergt. when I left Delville Wood, and daresay I should have had the full rank, if I hadn't been so fatheaded to get wounded.... Look here old man, don't you go knocking yourself up with those bally old accounts, your health is more important than them. Well I can't think of any more just now so will close.
With best love, Yours Ever, Pud.

Knotty Ash, L'pool   11–1–17

Dear Hal,

Many thanks for your letter. No the operation did not come off, and I am just about getting fed up with them..... Wilf is coming tomorrow and we are to have a game of chess together, I expect he will wipe me up, but I've been having a good many games lately. That was the chap I was trying to find when I was out in France, (Cecil Norton's brother), I'm glad he has had a leave at last. I was glad to hear news of the old 18th. I was wondering how they had come through, but I'm afraid there aren't many of the old boys left.... Well I don't think you have much cause to grumble at Clementine do you? I think she has done splendidly, considering what time you have spent on her. Well Hal old man will "Na, pooh" now hoping you are in the pink.
With best love, Yours Ever, Pud.

**Harold and Clementine
the motorbike.**

The next letter is particularly interesting because it mentions a contemporary incident which was to bring the Cromer Lifeboat Coxswain Henry Blogg one of his three gold medals. The wrecks were those of the *Pyrin* and *Fernebo*; the latter vessel broke in two after hitting a mine. Troops stationed in Cromer also played an important part in the rescue and brother Harold and father Robert were both probably involved as shore helpers, being leading members of the St. John Ambulance.

Knotty Ash, L'pool 17812   17–1–17
Dear Pa,
Very many thanks for your interesting letter. I should like to have seen those ship wrecks, it must have been very exciting.... I am getting along as usual and have not had the operation yet.... Well Pa I hope you are all serene at home, I'm soon going to do a bunk out of this hospital, it's nearly time I came home.
With best love, Your loving son, Raymond.

17812   19–1–17
Dear Hal,
Very many thanks for your letter.... I've been pinching out a lot now lately, although I'm supposed to be a bed patient, you bet I don't stay in bed all day. Well Hal I've not been under the operation yet, but another piece of bone worked out this morning, would you like it, to go with the other? Please excuse the horrible scribble but am writing it in bed. Must close now.
With best love to all, Yours Ever, Pud.

Knotty Ash, L'pool 17812   26–1–17
Dear Hal,
Very many thanks for your letters.... My leg is just the same, and am still waiting. We had another concert yesterday with "George French" up to entertain us, I don't know whether you have ever seen him, he's great. We haven't had a convoy for some time now, and three out of eight blocks are empty. Well Hal I've nothing to jaw about this week so will close. Hoping you are in the pink.
With best love to all, Yours Ever, Pud.

17812 Knotty Ash, L'pool   30–1–17
Dear Pa,
Very many thanks for your letter. Very sorry to hear about cousin Clarissa, I didn't know her. I have developed a rotten cold and am not feeling up to much at present. Is Sidney Kirby out of the army then? I suppose he didn't say how Charlie was! Wilf is coming up on Thursday or Saturday so he wrote and told me. My leg is still the same. I don't feel fit enough to write any more so will close.
With best love, Your loving son, Raymond.

The following letter is included here because of its interesting reference to the liner *Olympic*. The letter is undated and may have been written later in the year.

Knotty Ash, L'pool 17812
Dear Pa,
Many thanks for your letter and also the note which arrived all serene. The "Olympic"(I don't know whether I have spelt it right) the White Star Line, came into L'pool yesterday with 7,000 Canadians aboard. She is armed with six, six–inch guns, four in the bows and two in the stern, so you can guess she looks like a battleship instead of a liner....
Hoping all at home are well.
With best love to all, Your Affec. son, Raymond.

106

Knotty Ash, L'pool   7–2–17

Dear Hal,

Very many thanks for your letter. No I didn't have the operation.... Yes! I think the Huns have just about come to the end of the string, but I don't think it will make much effect on "Wilson".... Well Hal I'm like you, hung up for news so will have to dry up.
With best love to all, Yours Ever, Pud.

Knotty Ash, L'pool   16–2–17

Dear Hal,

Many thanks for your last letter. I duly received the war saving paper and signed and sent it off. I got a decent pair of boots for 25/–, but expect I could have got the same pair in peace time for 15/–. ... The doctors don't know what to make of my leg, I think they are going to x–ray it. I am just about to be dressed so will dry up.
With best love to all, Yours Ever, Pud.

Knotty Ash, L'pool   2–3–17

Dear Hal,

Many thanks for your letter.... They have started clearing the hospitals out up here, ready for the coming push, I expect I shall be just in time for it!... I haven't anything much to jaw about, so will close, hoping you are in the pink.
Yours Ever, Pud.

Knotty Ash, L'pool   8–3–17

Dear Hal,

Very many thanks for your letter.... I went and saw Stephenson v Reece in the billiard match, and saw Stephenson make a 473 brake (sic). I am going to see the "Bing Boys" on Saturday of course shall have to take a little extra time but that can't be helped. ... I wonder how Reg. Moulton likes the front line! The leg shows signs of improvement and I now walk without the slightest limp, but shall have to practice my old limp when I get back to the depot. Please excuse pencil but some of the other chaps have collared the only pen. With best love to all,
Yours Ever, Pud.

Knotty Ash, L'pool   16–3–17

Dear Hal,

Many thanks for your letter. I say! the blighters haven't pinched you for the army, have they? They ought to be blinking well shot if they have... I don't know what the dickens is going to happen if they pinch you for the army, they ought to be content with four of us in it.... I'm afraid there isn't many of the old 10th left, I have never come across any of them up here.... Well Hal I hope you are keeping fit and sincerely hope you will scrape through and not have to go up, of course I know how much you are wanting to go and do your bit, but I think you are doing more than your share at home and your job is a jolly sight harder than ours. Well I must close now old chap, as am run dry.
With best love to all, Yours Ever, Pud.

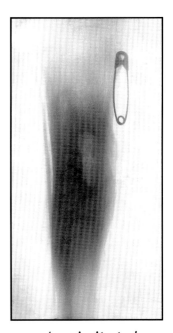

A curiosity to have survived amongst the papers is a set of x-rays taken of Ray's leg between August 1917 and February 1918.

Knotty Ash, L'pool   20–3–17
Dear Hal,
Many thanks for your letter, I think we have just got Fritz going, I hope he doesn't stop until he reaches Berlin. I'm jolly glad to hear they won't pinch you for the Army just yet....Well Hal haven't any news just now so will close.
With best love to all, Yours Ever, Pud.

Knotty Ash, L'pool   13–4–17
Dear Hal,
Many thanks for your letter and parcel which arrived all serene. Yes! I think old Fritz is getting it properly in the neck now, and I hope they will soon get near enough to bash a few German towns in. Could you let me know when Spring starts I think we must have missed a month. We have to go to bed in the bally daylight now, or should I say we are supposed to, I am usually out or walking round the grounds. Of course we have to make the beds look as though we are in them, but that's only a detail. We had a good laugh the other night, it was this way, one of the chaps was staying out a bit late, so he asked us to fake his bed up, so it wouldn't be noticed. So we put three bowls in it, well everything went alright until he came back. Then the silly blighter got into bed without removing the bowls and of course they rolled out of bed and kicked up the dickens of a row. Well the night nurse arrived on the scene but everyone was fast asleep and she hasn't found out yet who was rolling bowls round the ward. Well Hal I haven't anything much to write so will dry up. Hoping you are keeping fit.
With best love to all, Yours Ever, Pud.

Knotty Ash, L'pool   Friday
Dear Hal,
Thanks muchly for your letter and P.C... They have just taken off the guard so we are having the time of our lives, I hope they won't put on another one. ... Yes! I think Fritz's number is properly nailed up now, and the rotten war looks as though it might be over this year..... Well Hal can't write much this morning there's too much singing going on so will close.
With best love to all, Yours Ever, Pud.

Knotty Ash, L'pool   25–4–17
Dear Hal,
Many thanks for your letter. They have at last extended the hours which are now from 2p.m. to 6p.m., not that it makes any difference to me, because I make my own extension. We can get out any old time now the guard has gone, of course we could when the guards were here, but the faint hearted patients get out now. Ye guard has gone to munitions or rather to guard the works, which I think is a bit more useful than guarding hospital patients.... Am going on as per usual and am in the pink, hoping you are the same.
With best love to all, Yours Ever, Pud.

S'Knotty Ash, L'pool   7–5–17
Dear Hal,
*Many thanks for your letter and Reg's. Have been leading a gay time now lately and
they are just about getting fed up with us, our block has the famous name of being the
worst block in the hospital. We, my chum and I, slipped out after lights out the other
night and of course my chum didn't make his bed up properly and the night sister smelt
a rat and discovered our beds had dummies in them. So of course up we had to go in the
morning to be introduced to Dr. Hastings once again, we spun the yarn that we couldn't
sleep so we got up and had a walk round the grounds, and so far we have got off all
right. I was sorry to hear about Dick Cox, it will be very hard for his wife and kiddies....
Well Hal must dry up now.*
With best love to all, Yours Ever, Pud.

Knotty Ash, L'pool   13–5–17
Dear Hal,
*Many thanks for your letter. I am enclosing another piece of my tibia, which worked out
yesterday, it will do to match the others. I saw Sam Durrant's brother yesterday he's a
Sergt. and in hospital quite close to me. I happened to spot him in the Theatre yesterday
afternoon, he's been 11months in hospital down south and just been transferred up
here.... Yes! it's rotten all those casualties amongst the Cromer chaps. Well old chap am
still all serene and hope you are going well.*
With best love to all, Yours Ever, Pud.

Knotty Ash, L'pool   17–5–17
Dear Hal,
*Many thanks for your letter.... I have been thinking of getting engaged, but L'pool is so
far from home, I don't think it will be worth it?... Well Hal you know my letters are
always long so you must excuse this one being short.*
With best love to all, Yrs. Ever, Pud.

Knotty Ash, L'pool   23–5–17
Dear Hal,
*Many thanks for your letter and snap of Theo.... Well Hal! about my engagement, I
admit it was a bit casual the way I wrote about it, but I should like your advice. You
see I met this young lady about 3 months ago and, I like her very much, and I think she
likes me well enough to get engaged. But the question is, the distance from home, would
it be fair to tie her up, when perhaps after I go I shouldn't be able to see her for a long
time.... Well Hal I can't think of anything else so will dry up.*
 With best love to all, Yours Ever, Pud
P.S. Don't let all the family read this.

Knotty Ash, L'pool   26–5–17
Dear Hal,
*Many thanks for your letter and the note, which I received all serene.... Thanks very
much for your advice, I think it is the best thing to do, so I shall follow it..... Well Hal
haven't much to write this time except that my leg is going on a treat now, and have just*

had a dose of Silver Nitrate on it. Keep the photo dark when you get it, compre! (sic).
Must dry up now, hoping you are in the pink.
With best love to all, Yours Ever, Pud.

Knotty Ash, L'pool   29–5–17
Dear Pa,
Many thanks for your letter. I haven't yet heard anything of my transfer, but of course
there's sure to be a lot of red tape before it goes through... The doctor has just booked
me for an operation on Saturday but I am going to refuse it, on account of my getting
transferred it will mean another month or two in bed, if I let him slash me about, and I
can just as well have the op. at home. Well Pa haven't any more news just now so
will close.
With best love to all, Yours Affect. Raymond.

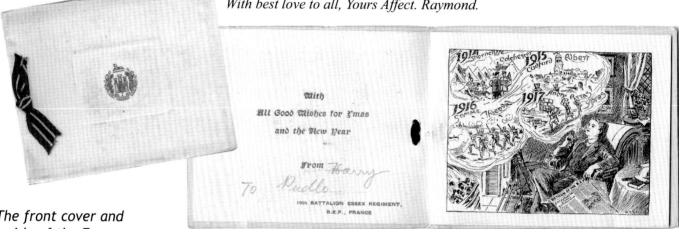

The front cover and
inside of the Essex
Regiment card for
Christmas 1917. The
back of the card
indicates that it was
sent by hospital friend
Harry Platt, apparently
back in the trenches.

Ray back home at
Colne House, Cromer.
The photograph was
probably taken after
his further operation
at the hospital in
Norwich as he is soldier
sitting in the right
hand bed.

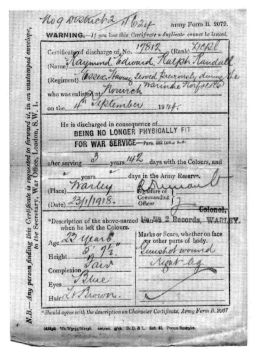

On June 2nd 1917 Ray was transferred to Colne House Royal Convalescent Home, Cromer.

In early October Ray was moved to "17 Ward (Main) War Hospital, Thorpe Norwich" for a further operation on his leg. During his time there he received the news that Reg Moulton, a good friend of all the family, had been killed.

Ray wrote his last letter from the hopsital in Norwich on 21st January 1918, indicating that he was expecting to return to Cromer in a few days.

On the 23rd January 1918 Ray was discharged from the army, being "medically unfit for further duty." Apart from the wound which was with Ray for the rest of his life and required continual dressing,

Brothers Hal and Ray, during Ray's convalescence at Cromer.

Petit Pierre.

there was another poignant reminder of his last desperate days in the war; the new family kitten was named "Delville".

Ray had said he "never wished to see France again". In the course of the initial research for this book in 1985, I went to the village of Longueval, on the edge of Delville Wood. With me I had the photograph of Petit Pierre, found with the letters. The then caretaker of the Commonwealth War Grave recognised the family name on the back of the photo. He spoke to the younger brother of Petit Pierre, the boy in the tub, who remembered a copy of the photograph in their family album. His mother had told him that it was taken by an Englishman injured in Delville Wood and he had sent her a copy. It seems that about 1930 Ray and some 10th Essex comrades did go back.

Ray worked in the family business for the rest of his life, alongside brothers Harold and Theo. They were all electricians and Ray repaired all sorts of electrical items, radios in particular. My own memories are of the rows of accumulator batteries along the shelves in his workshop, recharging ready for return to their owners. Brother Theo became a watch specialist and captain of the local fire brigade. Harold had been kept at home during the war to help his father run the business, but was called up at the end of the war to serve in the newly–formed R.A.F. for a short while. He was the clock repair specialist in civilian life.

Ray married and had two children; his brothers all had families and it was in one of the family homes that these documents were discovered after he and Harold had died. They were in a suitcase under a bed. Ray had never told his own children of his time at war.

Ray Randall, Cromer, circa 1935.

Index

1st Norfolks 30, 31, 45

2nd Norfolks 31

2nd Bedfordshires 67

5th Norfolks 6, 10, 23, 28, 40

6th Norfolks 31

6th Royal Berkshires 53

7th East Kents 31

8th Norfolks 5, 7, 10, 16, 24, 26, 33, 45, 48, 65

8th Suffolks 5, 7, 16, 25, 31, 34, 37, 43, 48

9th Division 86, 87

10th Essex Regiment 3–10, 16, 17, 19, 21–23, 25–35, 37, 38, 40, 42, 47–51, 56, 59, 62, 65, 66, 72–74, 76, 77, 79, 84 ,85 ,86, 88, 89, 90, 95, 111, 114,

10th Essex War Diary (National Archives) 28–35, 37, 40, 42, 50, 51, 56, 66

11th Royal Fusiliers 62

XIII Corps 78

15th Lancashire Fusiliers 48

15th Lancs. Fusiliers War Diary (National Archives) 48

16th Lancashire Fusiliers 48

18th Division 5, 40

19th Lancashire Fusiliers 45, 47

19th Lancs. Fusiliers War Diary (National Archives) 48

20th (King's) Liverpool Regiment 62

35th Division (Bantams) 84

51st (Highland Division) 21, 40

53rd Infantry Brigade 24

79th Company Royal Engineers 74

152nd Infantry Brigade 21

A

A.P.1 66

A.S.C. 45
Abbs, "young" 61
aeroplane 14
Agricultural Hall, Norwich 7
Allen, Fred, "Loady" 84
Amiens 21
armoured cars (tanks) 98
Army and Navy Gazette 15
Army, Regular 10, 19, 80
Army Service Corps 45
Authuille 23

B

B.E.F 24
Banks, Lieut. Col. T.M. and Chell, Captain
  R.A. *With the 10th Essex in France* 19,
  25, 38, 47, 73, 80, 85, 86
Bapaume 32
Bastow, Norman 69
bayonet 13, 14, 18, 19, 23, 50, 52, 84
Becourt Avenue 51
Berkshire Avenue 51
Bernafay Wood 86
Bertangles 21
Bethnal Green 8
Billon Wood 72
Bing Boys 107
Bisurated Magnesia tablets 68
Blighty 72, 101
Blogg, Coxswain Henry 105
Bly, "Lifter" 65
Blythe, Jack 84
bombardment 75
Boulogne 21
Bouzincourt. 21

Bray 25, 63, 69, 73
British Expeditionary Force 24
Bronfay Farm 63, 66, 72
Byerley, 2nd Lieut. 55
Buire 30, 31, 41, 42

C

Carnoy 25, 72, 74, 75, 84, 87
Caterpillar Wood 80, 87
Chell, R.A., Lieut., Adjutant. 80
Christmas Day 50
cinema, divisional 36
Citadel 26, 28
Clacton–on–Sea 11
Clementine (motorcycle) 24, 30, 34, 36, **45**,
  68, 102, 105
Codford St. Mary 15–19
Colchester 10, 11,43, 62, 63
  – Hyderabad Barracks 10–15
Colne House 89, 110
Corbie 50, 72
Cox, Dick 109
Cromer 13, 99
  – Colne House 89, 110
Cromer Post (newspaper) 23, 30, 44, 64, 96,
  97

Ray's service record, issued on his final discharge from the army in January 1918.

D

Daisey Dorma 100
Daniels, "young" 97
Daours 24, 50
Dardanelles 53
Davison, "young" 66
Delville, Delville Wood 39, 111
Douie, Charles *The Weary Road: The
  Recollections of a Subaltern of Infantry*
  42

dug–outs 47
Durrant, Sam 109

E

Egypt, Egyptian 6, 15, 23, 53, 74
Essex 8
Essex Regiment 10th Battalion, The, 8, 10, 16,
    21, 24, 33, 34, 50, 55, 58, 62, 73, 74, 78,
    81, 84, 86, 87, 94
Etinehem 62, 63, 66, 67
Evening News 96

*The 10th Essex
Regimental Band.*

F

Fernebo 105
field punishment 19
Fletcher, Pvt. O. 14877 25
Fokker 66
Folkestone 21
Franvillers 61
French, George 106
Froissey 69
Fusiliers 49, 51–53, 65

G

Garden of Sleep 61
Gee, Mr and Mrs 57, 65, 95
George V, H. M. King, 11, 18, 19, 40, 41
Gethen, Rev. L. 93, **94**
Gloucesters 7
Gough, Hubert 16

Grapes Hill 53
Gray, Sergt. 84
Grovetown 84

H

Hamilton, Rev. W. F. J. 69
Happy Valley (north of Bray) 26
Hardy, Mr 62
Harrison's Nursery Pomade 68
Harwich 12
Hastings, Dr. 109
Heilly 51
Highfield Military Hospital 89, 91, 92, 100
Hodges, Colonel's servant 80
Hollesley Bay 13
Hudson, 2nd Lt. 33
Hunt, Russel 66
Hyderabad Barracks 10–15

I

Icyclone 46, 47, 61, 66
Ilot , The 32, 33, 37
Ingersol(l) 42, 58, 60, 62, 66
Iodine 47, 68, 69
Ipswich 13

J

Jefferies, "young" 49, 66
Jefferies, Sergt. 83
Jordan, "young" 92

K

Kasino Point 80
Kelly, Mr and Mrs 97, 102,103
King, H.M. George V, 19, 40, 41
Kingsgate 55
Kirby, Charles 42, 50
Kirby, Sidney 31, 35, 106
Kitchener, Lord 5, 17, 19, 31
Knotty Ash 89
Koch, Herman, Musketeer 81

L

La Boisselle 32, 45, 48, 58
Lachrymatory (tear gas) shells 69, 75
Leyton 8
Liverpool, L'Pool 89, 91, 101, 102
        – Highfield Military Hospital 89, 91,

92, 100
– Knotty Ash 89
Lochnagar
– Sap 60
– Street 55
Longpré 72
Longueval, Longueval Alley 86, 87
Love, Fred 65

M

Mametz 55, 79
Manningtree 12
Maricourt 62–64, 66, 67, 72, 73, 87
Maxse, Lt Gen Sir Ivor 5, 10, 13,16, 40, 61,
        80
mines (explosive) 27, 61
Molliens-au-Bois 21
Montauban, Montauban Ridge 78, 79, 81,
        87, 88
Motorcycles (Magazine) 96
Moulton, Con 10, 36
Moulton, Reg 99, 107, 111
Mousehold, Mousehold Heath 31

N

National Archives 3
Nichols, Capt. G.H.F. Nichols *The 18th
        Division in the Great War* 7, 8, 40,
Nockels, "Loady" 65
Norfolk 5, 8, 53, 61, 95, 103
Norfolks 9, 31, 63, 84, 89, 90
Norfolk Football Annual 75
Norfolk Yeomanry 12
Northrepps 61
Norwich 7, 9, 19, 31
        – Agricultural Hall 7
        – Grapes Hill 53
        – Mousehold, Mousehold Heath 31
        – War Hospital, Thorpe 111

O

Olympic, S.S. 106
Outpost Duty 13

P

Parker, Tommy 37, 102
periscope 14

Petit Pierre 111
Platt, Harold 99
Picture Palace 36
Pommiers Redoubt 78
Poplar 8
Poincaré, Raymond (President of France) 40,
        41
Pyrin 105

R

R.A.M.C 61
R.F.A. 25
Radcliffe, Lieut. Col. J.F. 55
Randall, Clara 5, 6, 49, 71
Randall, Enid, "Jammy" 71
Randall, Harold, "Hal" 3, 5, 6, 9–19, 24, 26,
        30, 33, 35–37, 39,–45, 48, 49, 51,
        53–55, 57, 58, 60, 62, 64–75, 80–82, 84,
        87, 92, 95–111
Randall, Raymond, "Pudlo" 3–7, 9–17, 19, 21,
        23–25, 27–31, 33, 35, 37–44, 46–51,
        53–55, 57–58, 60–61, 63–82, 84, 86–87,
        89–104, 106–107, 110–111
Randall, Reginald, "Reg" 5, 6, 12, 24–26, 29,
        34, 36, 37, 40, 43, 46, 54, 57, 62, 65, 67,
        74, 81, 93, 95–103, 105, 109
Randall, Robert Laurence, "Pa" 5, 6, 13, 14,
        15, 19, 23, 25–27, 29–31, 33, 35, 36, 39,
        41–44, 46, 49, 53, 54, 57, 58, 60, 61, 63,
        65, 67–70, 73, 74, 81, 86, 91, 92, 95, 96,
        98–104, 106, 110
Randall, Robert, "Bobbo" 58
Randall, Theodore, "Theo" 5, 6, 9, 10, 19, 23,
        29, 30, 33, 41–44, 47, 53, 54, 60, 65,
        67, 70, 71, 81, 96, 97, 101, 103–105,
        109, 111
Randall, Wilfred, "Wilf" 5, 6, 9, 13, 24, 25,
        41, 58, 70, 92, 98, 104–106
Rechabite Friendly Society 83, 97
Rechabite Magazine 99
Regular Army 10, 19, 80
Ribemont 31
Robinson, Pvt. J.E., 17807 25
Rook, George 66
Royal Field Artillery 25
Royal Army Medical Corps 61
Rouen 91
Rubempre 21

S

St. Albans 15
St. John Ambulance Division 69
Salisbury 15
Sailly 69
Salter, Ralph 61
sausages 29, **37**–41, 43, 64, 72
Scone Street (trench behind the Ilot) 37
Scott, Lt. Col. H.L. 78
Shorncliffe Camp 8
Sidestrand
        – Garden of Sleep 61
Somme, Battle of the 5
Somme, river 24, 31, 61, 77, 97
Southampton 91
Spinks, Miss 69
Spring Avenue (trench from Billon Wood to
        Carnoy) 72
Stokes mortar 80
Stonehenge 18
Stratford 8
Suffolk 8
Support and Resources 4
Swaffham 97

T

tanks 95, 97, 98
Thiepval 22, 23
Thirtle 54
Trônes wood 85
Tween, Captain 89

U

Usna Redoubt 49

V

Vecquemont 24
Verdun 77

W

Wales, Prince of (later Edward VIII) 40, 41
Walthamstow 8
Walker, Charlie 97
Ward, Lance Corporal Harry 58
War Diaries, 10th Essex (National Archives)
        3, 25
War Hospital, Thorpe Norwich 111
War Office 67

watch, watches 33, 35, 37, 39, 41–44, 55,
        58, 61, 66–68
Wellington Redoubt 28
Western Front 58
Wheeler, Pvt. Albert 15401 25, 39
Wills, Mr and Mrs (relations through
        brothers' marriages) 30, 34, 36, 38,
        45, 49, 54, 65, 66, 62
Wiltshire 13
Woodbridge 13

X

x-rays 107

Z

Zeppelins, Zepps, Zeps 12, 14, 26, 30, **38**,
        39, 49, 92, 98, 103